JAPANESE MYTHOLOGY
A TO Z

JAPANESE MYTHOLOGY
A TO Z

Jeremy Roberts

Facts On File, Inc.

Japanese Mythology A to Z

Copyright © 2004 by Jim DeFelice

Facts On File, Inc.
132 West 31st Street
New York NY 10001

Library of Congress Cataloging-in-Publication Data
DeFelice, Jim, 1956-
Japanese mythology A to Z / Jeremy Roberts.
p. cm.—(Mythology A to Z)
Includes bibliographical references and index.
ISBN 0-8160-4871-1
1. Mythology, Japanese—Encyclopedias. 2. Japan—Religion—Encyclopedias. I. Title.
BL2202.R63 2003
299′.56—dc21   2003044942

Facts On File books are available at special discounts when purchased in bulk quantities for businesses, associations, institutions, or sales promotions. Please call our Special Sales Department in New York at
(212) 967-8800 or (800) 322-8755.

You can find Facts On File on the World Wide Web at http://www.factsonfile.com

Text design by Joan M. Toro
Cover design by Cathy Rincon
Maps by Jeremy Eagle © Facts On File

Printed in the United States of America

VB Hermitage 10 9 8 7 6 5 4 3

This book is printed on acid-free paper.

CONTENTS

Acknowledgments

I would like to thank my editors at Facts On File, Anne Savarese and Dorothy Cummings, for their help, in addition to Jeff Soloway, Lauren Goldberg, chief copy editor Michael G. Laraque, Elizabeth Margiotta, and the FOF production team. I would like to thank as well the people and ancestors of Japan for their inspiration. My humble effort is unworthy of their majestic spirit.

INTRODUCTION

Where do we come from? What will happen to us when we die? How should we live our lives? We still ask these questions today. In fact, the desire to ask them may be one of the things that makes us human.

All societies ask these questions, but not every society answers them in the same way. In most ancient human societies, the means of answering these important questions was religion. One way that ancient religions tried to answer basic questions about life and what it means to be human was through telling stories, specifically myths. A myth, in the original sense of the word, is a story whose truth is unquestioned.

THE HISTORY SETTING

Because myths reflect the culture that produces them, it is often useful to know a bit about that culture when studying them. This is especially true in Japan, where a number of influences came together to produce a rich and complex set of myths, or mythology.

Ancient Japan

Archaeologists are still working to discover the very early origins of human culture in Japan. There is definite evidence of humans at least 30,000 years ago, but little information about these people has survived. Probably about 10,000 B.C. people whom we now call the JOMON were living in Japan. The name *Jōmon* ("rope-pattern") comes from a type of pottery they made. It looks as if rope was pressed onto it to make markings, or it was made by coiling strips of clay.

By the fourth century B.C., a new culture emerged in Japan. These people—named YAYOI, after the place where their homes were first found by archaeologists—grew rice and used copper and other metals that earlier inhabitants did not.

The gap between 10,000 B.C. and 300 B.C. is vast, and there is considerable debate among scholars about what happened during that time. They are not even sure where the Yayoi came from, though they can offer a good guess. Because of the metal objects and items such as mirrors associated with Yayoi excavations, archaeologists believe that the Yayoi came from China and KOREA, or traded with people who did. The exact nature of this immigration or trade is still being studied, as is the culture of the times. But the Yayoi people used sophisticated iron tools and had social and agricultural systems capable of sustaining large populations. Large populations almost always have complex religious and political systems, and this seems to fit with ancient Japan as well.

The Yayoi seem to have spread from areas in western Japan eastward. By A.D. 250–350, the inhabitants of the Nara plain in Japan built large burial mounds, called *kofun* in Japanese. Historians generally connect the growth and spread of these keyhole-shaped tombs with the spread of the YAMATO clan, a large extended family that was prominent in the Yamat region of Kyūshū, the main island of Japan, by the early centuries of the first millennium and controlled western and central Japan.

Archaeologists also point out that the *kofun* are similar to mounds in southern Korea. There are several possible reasons for this. One is increased trade between the two areas. Another is the conquest of Korea by the Japanese people. But many anthropologists outside of Japan accept what is known as the "HORSE RIDER THEORY," which was suggested by Egami Namio. According to this theory, invaders originally from China settled in Korea and then came to Japan. These people— who rode horses—subdued the early Yamato leaders and substituted themselves as the new rulers. Gradually they took over all of Japan, unifying the many small settlements.

Besides archaeological finds, there is support for this theory in early Japanese myths and legends. Horses, for example, begin to appear only in stories known from a certain time. There are parallels or similarities in some of the myths to events known or thought to have happened. Of course, by their very nature, myths are open to interpretation. It would be extremely misleading to base any historical conclusion on myths alone.

Dragons were just one of many mythological elements influenced by the arrival of Buddhism in Japan. *(Richard Huber,* Treasury of Mythological Creatures*)*

Wherever they came from, the Yamato kings or emperors gradually and steadily extended their rule over the Japanese islands through warfare and diplomacy. Rival states in the Japanese islands were generally organized according to clans or family structures. They were called *uji*, and an important function of each clan was to honor or venerate ancestral gods.

The religion of Japan's emperor and people is SHINTO. It involves the worship of different KAMI, which can be the spirits of ANCESTORS or the divine essence of natural elements and phenomena, such as the rain or a mountain.

To justify their control, the Yamato rulers associated their clan with a story about the beginning of the world that linked them to the gods who had created it. This CREATION MYTH, or story about the creation of the world, became central to the Shinto religion. Once writing was introduced in Japan, those ORAL TRADITIONS were recorded in the *KOJIKI* (Record of Ancient Things) and the *NIHONGI* (*Chronicles of Japan*, compiled in the eighth century).

The Introduction of Buddhism

The country unified under the Yamato clan was strong enough to invade Korea, but the major Asian power at the time was China. By the fifth century A.D. frequent contact between Japan and China brought many CHINESE INFLUENCES to Japan. This helped spread and introduce BUDDHISM, an important religion that had begun in India centuries before (see INDIAN INFLUENCE). Other Chinese belief systems, such as TAOISM and CONFUCIANISM, were also introduced to Japan. At the same time, Japan's government began to model itself along the Chinese model. It became more centralized and bureaucratic.

Medieval Japan

Over a period of several hundred years, beginning in the ninth century, the emperor's power was whittled away. First, powerful families or clans took over as regents, acting as assistants to the emperor and then concentrating their own power. Then, as the central government became weaker, rival families or groups began to assume more authority.

Conflicts between the emperor and powerful families led to a bloody civil war between the MINAMOTO and TAIRA clans at the end of the 12th century, culminating in a battle at Dannoura in 1185 that resulted in the annihilation of the Taira, also known as Heike. This period and especially these battles gave rise to many legends and popular stories in Japan.

In the era that followed, the shogun, or military leader of Japan, dominated the country, ruling as much in his own name as the emperor's. Although the emperor and his family lost temporal power, his direct connection to the most important gods in the Japanese Shinto pantheon meant that he retained an important role in society. Others could usurp his authority or rule in his name, but they could not replace him. Nor could they take his place in religious ceremonies. This unique position helped ensure that the imperial family survived the tumultuous times. But it helped the society as well, giving it continuity and meaning. Japanese traditions—many deeply connected to myth—also survived with the imperial family.

The period from 1185 to 1868 was dominated by three different shogunates, or military regimes, periods when different families or clans dominated Japan: the KAMAKURA Shogunate (1192–1333), the Ashikaga Shogunate (1338–1598), and the Tokugawa Shogunate (1603–1867). The years between the shogunates were times of great disruption, confusion, and civil war.

In a feudal society, very specific roles are defined and passed on from birth. At the top of the Japanese feudal order was the emperor, followed closely by the Shogun, the greatest warlord in the country. Beneath him were the *daimyo*, lords who had great wealth and controlled large domains. Lesser lords rounded out the feudal aristocracy. Beneath them were samurai, warriors who for the most part were not noble and did not own land (though there were a few notable exceptions). The samurai are greatly celebrated in legends for their fighting ability, but during the later feudal period many worked as administrators and bureaucrats—performing what today we might call "desk jobs."

The most numerous class by far were farmers, ranked locally generally according to their wealth. Merchants and artisans were officially at the bottom of the local hierarchy, but in fact enjoyed a much higher standard of luxury than farmers and day laborers. Villages usually had a local government, with many decisions being made by village elders and headmen, who would deal with the local *daimyo*'s representatives.

The West

Europe played no role in Japanese culture until the arrival of Portuguese and other traders in the 16th century. After a brief period during which missionaries brought CHRISTIANITY to the islands, trade and contact with the West was severely limited. Relations were not established with major Western countries until the United States threatened Japan with force in 1854.

Japan's role in Asia gradually increased in the late 19th and 20th centuries. It fought a war with Russia in 1904–05 and took a small part in World War I. In the 1930s it became aggressively imperialistic, invading China and other countries. Eventually it went to war with the United States and the Allies in World War II. After the war, the Japanese government was reorganized under U.S. occupation. This ended the emperor's direct role in government, though he remains an important ceremonial figure in Japan today.

Japanese myths developed and changed as the country did. As we look at this evolution, it is important to remember that it was very complex. Examining the surviving myths is akin to looking at a series of snapshots rather than a long, consistent narrative movie.

RELIGIOUS TRADITIONS IN JAPAN

Kami

At the heart of very early Japanese religious practices are *kami*. The word is usually translated into English as "gods" or "deities," though the concept is actually more complicated than that.

Kami can be divided into two main categories. The first relate to natural phenomena. For example, a mountain or a stream may be thought to have a *kami* associated with it. A mountain *kami* might be seen to help a farmer by providing water during the growing season. This kind of spirit or force does not necessarily serve humans, but its favor can be beneficial to them. The opposite is also true—an angry *kami* can cause great destruction.

The second category of *kami* are ancestral spirits, called *uji-kami*, or clan deities. These spirits can help individuals in the present. However, they do much more than that. The process of honoring one's ancestors helps unify the extended family that descended from them. Maintaining these bonds strengthens the clan and the entire society. A person is responsible to these spirits for his or her behavior. If a person does something dishonorable, such as committing a crime or telling a lie, the ancestors are shamed as well.

The structure of society—with leaders or king at the top and "regular people" at the bottom—was also reflected in the *kami* structure. The more powerful *kami* could help an entire village or area.

No *kami* is all-powerful or flawless. Often in Japanese myths, the *ujikami* (*ujigami*) do things that a human might, getting into trouble or upsetting others. In this way, they are like Greek or Roman gods.

In early Japan, SHRINES to the *kami* were generally not very elaborate, nor were most prayers or rituals addressing them. Those in charge of the local government were also in charge of maintaining shrines and conducting the rituals honoring the important clan ancestors. Religion and government were, therefore, intertwined in the social structure. Ancestral *kami* shrines were kept by certain members of the clan entitled or allowed to do so. But anyone could pray to a *kami*, whether the deity was an ancestral god or one connected with a natural phenomenon.

SHAMANS, who could communicate with *kami* and use supernatural power to cure people, were an important part of early Shinto practices. The majority of these shamans were women. Certain families passed on the role of shaman from generation to generation. They had special procedures and rituals for contacting the dead as well as invoking the gods.

An ancient Japanese history states that there are 8 million *kami*, using a phrase that means "eight hundred times ten thousand," in the same way we might say "countless" or "millions and millions." While the figure may not have been meant literally, there are more *kami* than anyone can count. It is not an exaggeration to say that every village had its own special god forces and spirits that protected it. Every family venerated its ancestors. And stories or myths of those who had gone before

Special gates called torii signal the entrance to Shinto shrines. *(From Isabell L. Bird,* Unbeaten Tracks in Japan, *1880)*

were an important way for the families not only to remember the past but to show their place in the present.

The Shinto Pantheon

Although *kami* are numerous and varied, a few of these deities are especially important figures in Shinto mythology. The principal deities of the Shinto pantheon are:

- IZANAGI AND IZANAMI, the first gods, who created the world and many other gods
- AMATERASU, the sun goddess and heaven's ruler, whose grandson became the first emperor of Japan, according to tradition
- TSUKI-YOMI, Amaterasu's brother, the god of the Moon
- SUSANO-WO, the storm god and brother of Amaterasu. His feud with his sister caused him to be banished from heaven
- NINIGI-NO-MIKOTO, the grandson of Amaterasu who was sent to rule the earth

Buddhism

Buddhism originated in India during the fifth and sixth centuries B.C. Founded by Siddhartha Gautama, the Buddha, or "Enlightened One" (known in Japan as SHĀKA), the religion recognized that to be human means to suffer. To escape suffering one must renounce desires and follow an EIGHTFOLD PATH of righteousness. These eight principles call for a Buddhist to think, act, resolve, speak, work, strive, talk, and concentrate in the right manner. Only by doing this may a soul reach Nirvana, or ENLIGHTENMENT. Enlightenment is defined in different ways. We might think of it as an escape from the endless cycle of REBIRTH or as an unending state of bliss and peace.

Buddhism spread from India to many other countries, reaching China in the first century A.D. From China it reached Korea and then Japan by or in the sixth century. By that time, there were many different sects, or forms, of Buddhism. The sects emphasized different teachings from BUDDHA and about him. Gradually they came to have different attitudes about the nature of the universe and how enlightenment might be reached. While they agreed on many points, the differences set the sects apart.

The most important form of Buddhism for Japan followed the teachings of a school known as MAHĀYĀNA, or "Greater Vehicle" or "Greater Vessel," BUDDHISM. One of the central teachings of this school is that all creatures contain the innate Buddha. If a person can touch that innate character, he or she can gain enlightenment. But it is difficult—if not impossible—for most of us to do so without help.

Followers of Mahāyāna Buddhism believe that the historical Buddha was only one manifestation or incarnation of the everlasting Buddha or life force. According to Mahāyāna Buddhism, there have been many Buddhas, and there is always one Buddha in the world. These powerful beings have different "aspects," or characteristics, which emphasize certain qualities of the everlasting Buddha.

There are also a number of BODHISATTVAS, or Buddhas-to-be (BOSATSU in Japanese), who can help people achieve enlightenment. There are also a number of Buddhist gods and other beings that may be called on as well. Together, these represent an array of mythological figures. Their nature is complex, but most are able to present themselves in human or near-human forms.

This flexibility became very important when Buddhism was introduced to Japan in 552 (or 538; there are conflicting records). Since a Buddhist god could assume many forms, it eventually seemed natural to suggest that some *kami* were merely Buddhas or *bosatsu* in a different guise.

The Blending of Shinto and Buddhism

The Buddhist monk Kōbō DAISHI is usually credited with supplying the philosophy that allowed for the cooperation of the two religions. His theory was called RYŌBU-SHINTO, or "Shinto with two faces." Using this theory, it was possible to equate Shinto gods with figures from Buddhist mythology. For example, Amaterasu could be seen as the Japanese version of Vairocana, whose name means "sunlike." Vairocana is the all-powerful, sunlike manifestation of the everlasting Buddha. In this way, the most important Shinto god was seen as a version of the most important member of the Buddhist pantheon.

A similar idea was developed by the TENDAI sect of Buddhism. Its philosophy was called SANNŌ SHINTO. In Tendai Buddhism, the universal Buddha is seen as the central and most important figure. But, following the teaching of the *Lotus Sutra*, adherents of Tendai recognize that Buddha uses many different vehicles—lesser gods, scriptures, stories—to help others reach enlightenment. This idea encouraged syncretism, or the combining of different beliefs, in Buddhism and Shinto. It encouraged followers to look for parallels and make connections between the different gods and traditions.

The adoption of Buddhism by the SOGA clan, a leading family that was influential at the imperial court, helped win the religion's acceptance, but many fires and other disasters were blamed on the intrusion of Buddhist gods into areas held sacred by the Shinto *kami*. Finally in the mid-eighth century, Shinto priests from the Usa shrine, dedicated to HACHIMAN, took part in a ceremony to spread the *kami*'s protection to a Buddhist temple being built in Nara. Soon afterward, other *kami* were invoked to protect other TEMPLES.

Buddhists returned the favor. Hachiman—a Japanese mythic figure was declared a *bosatsu*, or a Buddhist mythic figure. With Buddhist influence on the rise, Buddhist teachers developed a theory that *kami* were unenlightened. They needed, therefore, to be helped to reach enlightenment by Buddhist influence. Temples were built near Shinto shrines to help make the process easier. Shinto shrines had grown increasingly elaborate during the Yamato period. The combination shrine-temples were even grander.

Strict lines might be drawn between the different gods by priests and other specialists. But for most people, the two different systems tended to blend. One could honor both *kami* and Buddhist figures. Being a Buddhist did not mean giving up Shinto.

The Buddhist Pantheon

It is impossible to make a statement about all of the members of the Buddhist pantheon, or collection of holy beings, that would either be comprehensive or satisfy all sects and practices. For general purposes, however, it is useful to group these entities into three broad categories: Buddhas, *bosatsu*, and kings or guardians.

In its most basic definition, "Buddha" simply means one who has become enlightened. All Buddhists believe that the founder of Buddhism achieved enlightenment. Most also believe that there have been others who have done so. The most important Buddha in Japan is AMIDA, a central figure for the PURE LAND sects. For believers, saying his name at DEATH deposited the soul in the Pure Land where enlightenment was possible.

Bosatsu, or "future Buddhas," are souls that have made themselves fully ready for enlightenment but have chosen to delay it so they may help others. (It should be remembered that the enlightenment of *bosatsu* is already guaranteed.) The most important *bosatsu* in Japan were FUDŌ, whom scholars believe was probably derived from a form of the Indian god Shiva; KANNON, the *bosatsu* of compassion; and FUGEN, the *bosatsu* of reason.

The natural beauty of Japan, as well as its Shinto heritage and Buddhist influences, combine to transform even ordinary things, such as a garden, into works of art. In one simple view, a skilled gardener can evoke nature and the gods in shimmering tranquility. *(Library of Congress, Prints & Photographs Division [LC-USZ62-094499])*

The last class of Buddhist deities includes what are sometimes called "fierce Buddhas" as well as kings and guardians. The fierce Buddhas do the fighting for the Buddhas. Five guard the compass points of heaven: east, west, north, south, and central. In Japan, these are referred to as MYŌ-Ō, representations of which are often seen guarding Buddhist temples or monasteries. There are also two lesser deities known as NIO or GUARDIAN KINGS who guard the temple gates and shrines.

There are not very many female gods anywhere in the Buddhist pantheon, with the exception of sects in the country of Sri Lanka, where Pattinī is celebrated as a major deity. This is a reflection of gender prejudices from the time, which placed males in a superior position in most of the societies where Buddhism developed.

The most important members of the Japanese Buddhist pantheon include:

- Amida, an important protector of humankind
- DAINICHI NYORAI, an important Buddha especially venerated in the Tendai and SHINGON sects
- Fugen, the *bosatsu,* or future Buddha, of wisdom and understanding
- Kannon, a *bosatsu* with several manifestations
- Fudo, a Myō-ō who does battle against avarice, anger, and folly
- JIZŌ, a *bosatsu* of great strength
- EMMA-O, the god of hell
- IDA-TEN, who watches over monasteries

Other Chinese Influences

While Buddhism played the most important role in Japanese mythology, there were other important Chinese influences on Japan during the Yamato era and the years following. For mythology, the most important of these were Confucianism and Taoism. Confucianism though not actually a religion, is a system of thought and ethics that exerted a strong influence over Japanese society and institutions. Taoism also came to Japan during the period of increased Chinese influence. The Tao, or "the Way," combines philosophy with ancient Chinese folk religion and superstitions. One of the central ideas of Taoism is that the way of the universe must be accepted; fate is inevitable, and one must bend to it like a young tree covered by ice in a windstorm. Also central to Taoism and Chinese thought in general is a belief that things are formed by two opposing forces, or yin and yang. The pairing of opposites, such as hot and cold or life and death, shape all reality. This idea is an important part of *onmyo,* a form of divination related to Taoism that came to Japan from China during this period. Wandering priests known as *onmyo-ji* studied omens and advised when the time might be good for different activities, such as getting married.

USING THIS BOOK

This book lists the major figures in Japanese mythology in alphabetical order, as in an encyclopedia. It also includes information about some of the most popular legends and a few folktales that readers may encounter as they begin to learn about Japan. Finally, a few important terms relating either to Japan or the study of myths are included to help the reader in his or her studies.

Cross-references to other entries are rendered in SMALL CAPITAL LETTERS. Some topics with entries in this book are known by more than one name. Alternate names are given in parentheses after the entry headword. Those given in full capital letters are variations of the names from the original language; those appearing in upper- and lowercase letters are English translations.

Lists of some of the important Shinto and Buddhist deities are included in the back of the book and might be useful to someone beginning to learning about the myths.

NOTES ON JAPANESE LANGUAGE AND PRONUNCIATION

Japanese and English are two very different languages, recorded in different ways. The English language is written in what is known as the Roman alphabet. The Japanese language uses *kana* and *kanji* syllabaries, or characters representing phonetic sounds. These have no relation to the ABC's most Westerners grow up with. *Kanji,* which developed from Chinese, is used to represent most basic Japanese words. One type of *kana,* known as *hiragana,* is used with *kanji* to show punctuation and refine meaning. Another type of *kana,* known as *katakana,* is generally used for foreign words, media headlines, and for some special uses, such as in children's books.

Translators have worked out a system to present the Japanese language to Westerners. The system uses Roman characters to reproduce the sounds of the words in Japanese. In theory, the transliteration is direct, but there are a few things to remember.

First of all, long vowels are usually represented with a long dash (macron) over them, just as they would appear in a standard English dictionary. Ō, for example, stands for the long *o* sound we hear in *go.* This convention is sometimes ignored for words that are very common in the West, such as Tokyo.

Consonants are mostly pronounced as they are in English, with a few exceptions:

- The "tsu" sound is difficult to render in English. It has the sound of a hard *t* followed by *z. The Random House Japanese-English Dictionary* (New York: Random House, 1997), written by Seigo Nakao, compares the sound to the combination in *footsore*
- "ch" always sounds like the *ch* in *church*
- "g" always sounds like the *g* in *go*
- "f" before *u* sounds more like the *h* in *holy* than what most English speakers would hear as an *f.* So Fudō's name starts more like *huh* than *fuh*
- An *r* tends to sound closer to *l* for English speakers than the *r* they normally hear (there is no *l* in Japanese). It is sometimes described as a soft *r* rather than the hard, rolling *r* common in the Americas

Because the Romanization system is based on sounds, and because pronunciation and interpretation can differ, there are many instances where a slightly different version might be accepted or preferred by some people. In other instances, new spelling conventions have replaced older ones, though not always consistently. Some of the differences are very minor. For example, some sources capitalize the *W* in Susano-Wo; others do not. Other differences are more noticeable: some sources render

Susano-Wo as *Susanoo*. When looking up a main entry, it may be best to keep the possibilities of variations in mind. O and *u* are especially interchangeable in the English renderings of Japanese terms.

I have tried to use as main entries those spellings a student is most likely to find and then listed the most likely variations. Admittedly, this is subjective.

Finally, some renderings of Japanese words in English use hyphens to separate parts of the words. Placing these hyphens is usually based on the way the original Japanese ideograms were written. Unfortunately, there is no agreed-on convention, and the result in English varies widely. Three sources citing the same word may render it three different ways, all of which are technically correct. Again I have tried to follow the usage I perceived as being the most common, but this was often arbitrary.

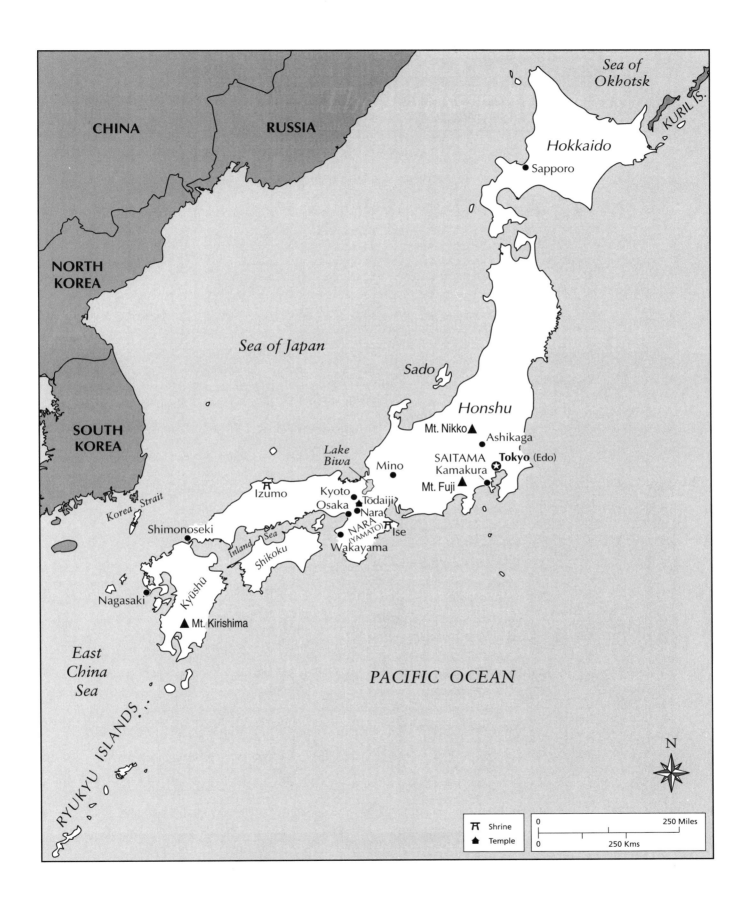

CHINA

RUSSIA

Sea of
Okhotsk

Hokkaido

KURIL IS.

● Sapporo

NORTH
KOREA

SOUTH
KOREA

Sea of Japan

Sado

Honshu

Mt. Nikko ▲
● Ashikaga

Lake
Biwa

● Mino

SAITAMA
Kamakura
● **Tokyo** (Edo)

⛩
Izumo

Kyoto ●
Osaka ●

Tōdaiji
● Nara

Mt. Fuji ▲

Korea Strait

NARA
(YAMATO)
⛩ Ise

Shimonoseki ●

Inland Sea

Shikoku

● Wakayama

Nagasaki ●

Kyūshū

▲ Mt. Kirishima

*East
China
Sea*

PACIFIC OCEAN

RYUKYU ISLANDS

N

⛩ Shrine
▲ Temple

0		250 Miles
0		250 Kms

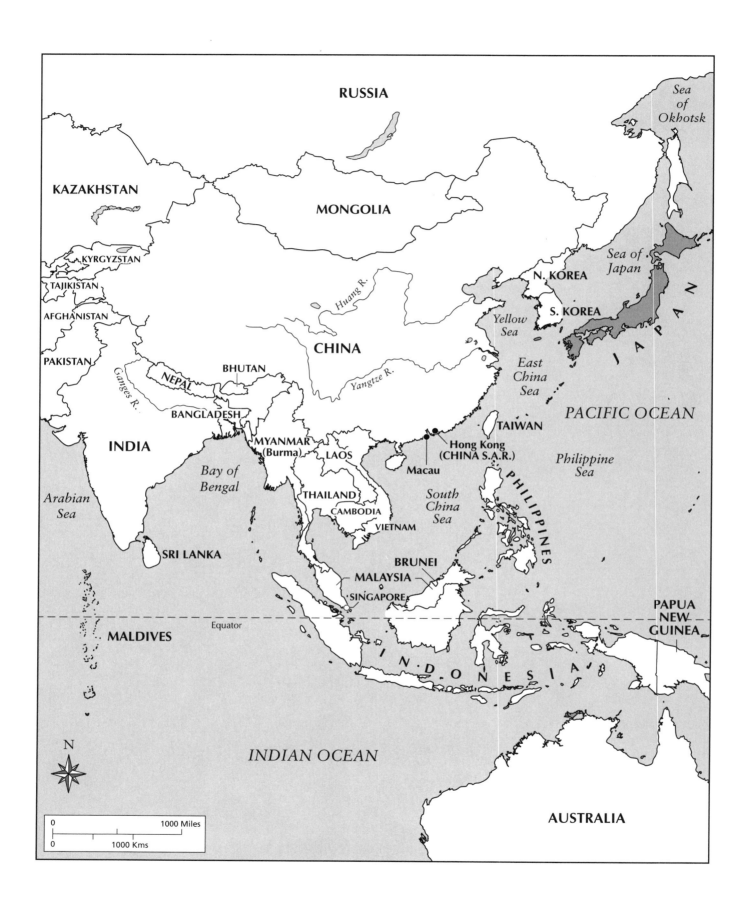

A-to-Z Entries

A

ABISHA-HŌ One of the best-known YORIGITŌ rituals, a Buddhist method for contacting the world of spirits. It dates from ancient times and was practiced in rural villages until the end of the 19th century.

AFTERLIFE The early SHINTO myths and legends do not define in detail what happens to people after they die. The main CREATION MYTH concerning the start of the world (see IZANAGI AND IZANAMI) refers to the land of the dead, known as YOMI, as a horrible, "unclean" place beneath the earth. Demons live there, and maggots feast on corpses. Many scholars believe that because Shinto connected death with impurity and a dismal state, people welcomed Buddhism, which had more positive associations.

In Japanese Buddhist tradition and myth, a person who dies is often pictured traveling across a wide open plain after death. A mountain rises at the end of the plain; the dead climb the mountain, then descend it to the banks of SANZU NO KAWA, the river of three crossings. There are three paths across the river. A person who did much good in his or her life can take a bridge. A mild sinner can wade across the shallow part of the water. Evil people must struggle across the deepest passage, harassed and held back by horrible monsters. When the dead reach the other side, an old woman waits to take their clothes and then send them on to god of the underworld EMMA-O. Emma-O judges them and sentences them to a part of the underworld where they will work out their sins before returning to be reborn.

While the Buddhist underworld is sometimes called hell, it differs from the Judeo-Christian concept significantly. The intervention of a BODHISATTVA can relieve a dead person of his or her punishment. In some ways, this part of the underworld is more like the Christian purgatory, where souls eventually work off their sins.

Early Shinto beliefs did not link the afterlife with punishments or rewards for things a person did while alive. Some experts on Japanese history and religion believe that the emphasis on consequences in the afterlife may have helped BUDDHISM spread in Japan. An afterlife where good deeds are rewarded and bad punished offers the living some consolation when a loved one dies or when they think about their own death. Perhaps for this reason, even today Buddhist rituals are more common at death than those directly related to Shinto.

Scholars also believe that because of the Buddhist influence, later Shinto legends and stories of the afterlife included references to punishment more in line with these ideas.

AGRICULTURE Farming was an important occupation in early Japan, and many myths relate to it. The most basic and ancient precepts often refer to it. For example, the linked concepts of purity and uncleanliness were central to Japanese culture, and the words expressing this concept have to do with agriculture. Something that is unclean or impure is *kegare* or "unable to make things grow." (*Ke* means "able to make things grow"; *gare* is "not" or "un.")

Of the many crops historically grown in Japan, none is more important than RICE. It remains an important part of the Japanese diet today. Rice did more than nurture the body in ancient Japan. It had a spiritual significance. Even today, offerings of rice are an important part of even the simplest rituals. Growing such a critical food source in ancient times was an important job, and rice farmers still have a special place in Japanese society.

There are several gods associated with farming or agriculture or different agricultural products or processes. Among them are DAIKOKU, TOYO-UKE-BIME, INARI, and YAMA-UBA.

AINU The Ainu are the oldest inhabitants of Japan whom anthropologists have been able to document and study in detail. Once widespread, they now are a small minority in the country. They live primarily on Hokkaido, the large island at the north of Japan, and the Kurile Islands.

Anthropologists have debated for many years precisely where the Ainu came from and how they are or are not related to other peoples who have lived on the Japanese islands. One set of recent theories favor a connection with the Jōmon culture, which extended throughout Japan until immigration from Korea and China ushered in a new era. (See JŌMON PERIOD.) Other theories separate the Ainu entirely from the Jōmon as well as from the Japanese who followed.

Whatever their origins, the Ainu were gradually confined to the north, as Japanese culture grew in the south. They preserved their local ways for centuries and remained in many ways distinct from the other inhabitants of what is now modern Japan.

As contact between the dominant culture and the Ainu increased, the Ainu were treated as inferiors. From roughly the 15th century onward, the island of Hokkaido was colonized by Japanese from the southern islands. Laws passed in the 1800s discouraged Ainu from following their ancestral ways. Policies of integration and suppression eventually left relatively few "pure" native people on Hokkaido. These policies remain very controversial, just as in America the treatment of native peoples has been and remains a matter of concern.

Physical as well as cultural and historical differences separate the two groups of people. Someone of "pure" Ainu descent may appear different from a "typical" Japanese. His beard, for example, is usually much fuller. He might have brown hair and eyes that seem a little more rounded than the eyes of a "typical" Japanese. Ainu are classified as "non-Mongoloid" to contrast them to their Japanese, Chinese, and other Asian neighbors.

The word *ainu* means "people" or "human" in the Ainu language. The Ainu have myths and legends that are different from those of the Japanese of the southern islands, reflecting their different experience. However, the Ainu religion is animistic, seeing divinity in all things, and in some ways may be similar to very early SHINTO.

According to the Ainu creation myth, the universe consists of six skies and six worlds. At the very top level lives Kamui the Great God. Below him live lesser gods. Demons inhabit the lowest level.

The underworld can be reached through a long cave. Anyone who eats food there is transformed into a snake. Evildoers are sent to hell, whose fires burn in the eruptions of volcanoes.

According to the Ainu creation myth, the universe existed as a slimy ooze on the back of a giant

This illustration from a book published in the United States at the end of the 19th century shows the traditional clothes worn by Ainu men in ancient times. *(From Isabell L. Bird,* Unbeaten Tracks in Japan, *1880)*

trout. The Great God sent a water-wagtail—a small water bird common in the region—to create the earth from the ooze. At first, the bird was not sure what to do. Finally it flapped its wings hard enough to pull mud from the muck, then shaped it into the earth by tramping it with its feet and tail.

The trout that holds the earth creates tides by sucking the water of the universe in and out. The fish is kept in place by two large divinities, who hold it so it cannot jump and violently upset the world on his back. Earthquakes occur when one of the gods finds it necessary to take a hand off the trout to eat.

The Ainu have a variety of other myths and legends, many pertaining to the animals common in the region where they live. The bear is especially venerated. Some Ainu are said to have descended from bears, and the animal is invoked in several rituals.

In the story of Poi-Soya-Un-Mat, a young hero named Otsam-Un-Kur hears about a woman named Poi-Soya-Un-Mat who dresses and acts like a man. He meets her while hunting. After a fight, Otsam-Un-Kur kills Poi-Soya-Un-Mat, but she is revived. The hero discovers that he is supposed to be married to her, a terrible prospect in his opinion, since this woman keeps acting like a man. Finally, Ostam-Un-Kur finds a submissive woman to marry.

In the story of Shinutapka-Un-Mat, a woman who is supposed to marry the foster brother who raised her is warned by a bear in a dream that he plans to murder her. When she wakes, the bear fights him and takes Shinutapka-Un-Mat away to her real brothers. The bear eventually returns as a god, taking Shinutapka-Un-Mat as his wife.

AIZEN-MYŌ-Ō   The popular Buddhist Japanese god of love. This love can be physical love, such as desire for another person. But in Buddhist theology, Aizen-Myō-ō represents love on a higher or intellectual plane. He reminds us that desire can be a powerful force for good. The love of knowledge or ENLIGHTENMENT, which Aizen represents, can be an important force in the world as well as for individual people.

Artists usually show Aizen with three eyes and a lion's head in his hair. He has six arms, and each arm holds a weapon. Though he looks like a ferocious warrior, Aizen has a great love for people and is very kind.

How ferocious can love be? Aizen's fierce face says very—and just try escaping his six arms! *(Richard Huber,* Treasury of Mythological Creatures*)*

As the word MYŌ-Ō indicates, Aizen is one of the kings of light, or *vidyarajas*, in BUDDHISM. Like the other *myō-ō*, Aizen is shown in art as a ferocious warrior. But his popular descriptions make his kindness obvious.

AJARI JOAN   Popular legends tell of Ajari Joan being a Buddhist priest on Hakkotsu-San, or Skeleton Mountain. While there, he fell in love with a girl, a violation of his oath of celibacy. Because of his sins he became an *okuma*, or devil, and destroyed his TEMPLE. Much later he came to his senses and devoted himself to prayer. He continued to pray— even after his death—and was transformed into a praying skeleton. The story can be interpreted as a metaphor: no matter how great your sin, it is possible to repent.

AJI-SHIKI   The SHINTO god who created Mount Moyama from the mortuary house, a kind of tomb, of his friend. Aji-Shiki was overcome by grief for his friend and cut the mortuary house down from heaven. The mountain was created where it fell.

AJI-SUKI-TAKA-HI-KONE   One of the SHINTO gods of thunder. Just as parents may carry a crying child up and down a hallway to soothe him or her, the gods carry Aji-Suki-Taka-Hi-Kone up and down a ladder to try and quiet him. This explains why the sound of thunder begins faintly, becomes louder, then fades.

AKUDŌ   According to Buddhist belief, these are the worst paths a soul may take when being reborn. This includes living in hell or becoming a GAKI, hungry spirit. Some say it is also possible to be born as evil giants known as ASURAS.

ALL-SOULS' DAY   A common Western description of BON, also called the Feast of Lanterns.

ALTAR   Many if not all traditional Japanese homes contain an altar where the different spirits and deities important to the individual family are commemorated. Both a SHINTO altar (*kamidana*) and a Buddhist altar (*butsudan*) are often used to honor spirits important to the family.

The *KAMI*, or deities, associated with the family ancestors stretch back literally hundreds of generations to the very early days of Japan. Other *kami* with special meaning to the family can also be honored at the altars.

It is helpful to remember that the early Shinto myths do not draw a line between the deities and "regular" people. Many people, especially in Japan, believe that humans descended from the gods. This divine connection is one reason why honoring ancestors is so important in many Asian societies.

AMA   The Japanese word for the upper dwelling place of the gods, or HEAVEN. In the SHINTO myths, some deities live in heaven and others dwell on earth. Unlike Christian versions of heaven, Ama is not an afterlife for souls who have died. A closer parallel is Mount Olympus in Greek mythology.

The word is often used as part of the name of Shinto deities who live in heaven, or to describe something related to them.

AMA-NO-MINAKA-NUSHI   The divine lord of middle heavens in SHINTO myths. The ancients identified him with the North (or Pole) Star.

AMA-NO-MURAKUMO-NO-TSURUGI   The sacred sword, also known as *hokēn,* that AMATERASU gave to her grandson when she sent him to rule the earth. It is one of the SANSHU NO JINGI, or three treasures of the emperor's divine rule, along with YASAKANI NO MAGATAMA (the jewel strand) and YATA NO KAGAMI (the mirror).

The sword was lost during the GEMPEI WAR but then replaced.

AMA-NO-UKI-HASHI   The floating bridge that connects heaven and earth in SHINTO mythology. Eight roads are traditionally believed to lead to all places on earth at the foot of the bridge. The bridge is guarded by a deity called the Guardian of the Bridge or Guardian of the Paths, SARUTAHIKO OHKAMI. He decides who shall pass and who shall not, and his decisions are not always automatic.

For example, when the sun goddess AMATERASU sent her grandson to rule the earth, the guardian blocked the way. The goddess UZUME came to persuade him to let the young man and his retinue pass. Uzume was so impressive that the guardian asked to marry her. She agreed, and from that day on lived with him at the bridge.

According to the ancient myths, the floating bridge collapsed to earth one day when all of the gods were sleeping. The jutting area west of Kyoto is said by some to be its remains. The *Tango-fudoki*—one of many books of customs and local descriptions the government ordered to be written in 713—records this story.

Some scholars studying the ancient myths believe the idea of a bridge between heaven and the earth may have been suggested by a rainbow.

AMATERASU   (AMATERASU-Ō-MIKAMI, Heaven Shining Great Deity) Amaterasu, the SHINTO goddess of the sun, is the most important divinity in the Shinto pantheon, or collection of gods. She is held to be the ancestor of the emperor and is the most revered person of heaven. But she is not all-powerful, and, in fact, the stories that describe her make her seem very human—though, of course, on a godly scale.

According to the Shinto CREATION MYTH, Amaterasu was born when Izanagi returned from his unsuccessful attempt to rescue his wife, Izanami (see IZANAGI AND IZANAMI), from YOMI, the land of the dead. Amaterasu emerged from one of his eyes. At the same time, a sister, the moon goddess TSUKIYOMI (who is male in some tales) and a brother, SUSANO-WO, were also born.

Izanagi gave Amaterasu his sacred beads (YASAKANI NO MAGATAMA) and told her she would rule over heaven. He then told Susano-Wo that he would rule over the seas. But Susano-Wo was jealous of his sister. He told his father that he would leave and go to YOMI to join his mother, Izanami. This made Izanagi very angry. He ordered Susano-Wo out of his sight.

Susano-Wo went to see his sister Amaterasu to say good-bye, but Amaterasu suspected a trick and kept her bow and arrows with her. Susano-Wo assured her he meant no harm. He protested that he did not want to take her rule away.

But he soon showed his jealousy. He suggested a contest to see who was more powerful. Whoever could create more gods would be the winner, he said.

Amaterasu began by breaking her brother's sword into three pieces and eating it. When she spit out the pieces, a mist formed in the air. Three goddesses formed from the mist.

Susano-Wo was unimpressed. He took his sister's beads and cracked them with his teeth. Five male gods appeared.

"I have won," he told Amaterasu.

"No," she answered. "The gods came from my jewels. I am the winner, since your poor sword produced only three gods, and they were all female."

Susano-Wo rampaged across the earth, claiming that he was the victor of the competition. He flooded RICE fields and caused great destruction. He even defiled the TEMPLE where the rice harvest was to be held by defecating in it. Finally, he took a pony and skinned it alive, then hurled the beast into a sacred hall where Amaterasu was weaving with her attendants. One of the maidens fainted dead at the sight.

Amaterasu fled to a dark cave, leaving the earth in darkness. She refused to come out. The world threatened to wither away in perpetual darkness, ruled by evildoers whose deeds were cloaked in the night.

Finally, the earth's good gods decided to trick Amaterasu into emerging. They set YATA NO KAGANI, made by Ama-Tsu-Mara and Ishi-Kori-dome, in front of her cave, along with the cock that crows before the dawn. Then they asked the goddess UZUME to dance for them in front of the cave. Uzume began slowly, but quickly found her rhythm. The somewhat plump goddess grew so happy that she threw off all her clothes, dancing wildly—which made all of the others laugh very hard.

Amaterasu heard the laughter and wondered what was going on. When she came to the mouth of the cave to investigate, she saw her reflection in the mirror. Curious, she asked who the beautiful goddess was. The other gods told her it was her replacement. Her own beauty entranced her, and she emerged slowly to examine the image. The world once more was bathed in sunlight.

Tajikawa quickly blocked the entrance to the cave so she could not return. With the return of light, the world regained its balance. Evil once more was put in its place.

Susano-Wo, meanwhile, was punished by the other gods. His beard and moustache were cut off. His fingernails were ripped away, and he was fined and banished from heaven. He wandered the earth and had several adventures. Finally, he slew an eight-headed serpent. When it died, a sword fell from its tail. Repenting of his feud with his sister, he sent the sword as a sign that he was submitting to her rule. The sword, called AMA NO MURAKUMO NO TSUGURI, is said to remain in the emperor's possession.

Emerging from the shadows, Amaterasu showed people how to grow rice and wheat, weave, and cultivate silkworms. Some say that she and her attendants wove and continue to weave the cloth of the universe.

Amaterasu later asked her son, Ame-No-Oshido-Mimi, to rule the earth. After he turned her down, she sent her grandson NINIGI-NO-MIKOTO. Japan's emperors trace their ancestry directly to Ninigi and, thus, to Amaterasu.

Many scholars point out that the fact that the most important divinity is female is very significant.

Some say this shows that women played an important role in early Japanese societies. The myth may present evidence that early Japanese rulers were female. Or it may mean that women priests or SHAMANS played an important political as well as religious role. In any event, the myth of Amaterasu contrasts greatly with many Western myths, in which females play subservient roles.

Amaterasu's full name is "Amaterasu-O-Mi-Kami," which might be literally translated as "the important being who makes heaven shine." She is also known as Amaterasu Omikami and Omikami ("illustrious goddess").

Amaterasu remains a very popular figure in Japan. Her SHRINE at Ise is the most popular and important in the country. Those visiting Ise at the time of the harvest festival remember the imperial family in their prayers, thanking the goddess for her protection and blessings.

AMATSU-KAMI (*AMUSU-KAMI*) In SHINTO mythology, *kami* (gods) who live in the sky or heaven.

AMA-TSU-MARA The god of blacksmiths. Ama-Tsu-Mara helped make the mirror that lured AMATERASU from her cave.

AME-NO-HOHI According to the SHINTO myths, Ame-No-Hohi was sent to rule the earth after Amaterasu's son Ame-No-Oshido-Mimi turned down the job. When he did not send word back for three years, the gods sent his son Ame-No-Wakahiko to look for him. Eventually, Amaterasu sent her grandson NINIGI-NO-MIKOTO to rule the earth.

AME-NO-MI-KUMARI A SHINTO water goddess.

AME-NO-OSHIDO-MIMI AMATERASU's son. He turned down the chance to become the ruler of the earth, saying that it was too filled with chaos. His son NINIGI-NO-MIKOTO was eventually sent in his place.

AME-NO-UZUME The full name of UZUME.

AME-NO-WAKAHIKO According to SHINTO mythology, Ame-No-Wakahiko is AME-NO-HOHI's son. After Ame-No-Hohi was sent to rule the earth,

the gods in heaven heard nothing from him for three years. Wondering what was going on, they finally convened and decided to send his son Ame-No-Wakahiko to find out.

Ame-No-Wakahiko was no better at communicating with the other gods than his father. He did, however, find true love on earth. He married the daughter of OKUNINUSHI, a Shinto god of magic and medicine. His wife's name was Shitatera-Hime.

After eight years passed without word from Ame-No-Wakahikio, the gods sent a pheasant to earth to see what was going on. Thinking the bird was an evil omen, Ame-No-Wakahiko shot at it as it sat on a tree near his house. The arrow traveled all the way to heaven. The sky god TAKAMI-MUSUBI recognized the arrow as one given to Ame-No-Wakahiko. Insulted because he thought the god was attacking heaven, he hurled it back. Ame-No-Wakahiko was killed.

AMIDA (AMIDA BUDDHA, AMIDA NYORAI) In Japanese BUDDHISM, Amida is the BUDDHA of boundless light. He is infinitely powerful and wise. Amida is one of five Buddhas of contemplation and by far the most popular or well-known among Buddhists.

Amida is the Japanese equivalent of Amitābha, as he is called by his Sanskrit name. According to legend, Amida was born from a LOTUS flower. He is also known as Amida-Nyorai and Amida Buddha.

Some Buddhists believe that Amida will grant them REBIRTH in a place called the "Pure Land," or Amitābha. This is a kind of heavenly paradise, but it does not represent the ultimate attainment of NIRVANA, or ENLIGHTENMENT. Instead, the soul may eventually achieve ultimate enlightenment by dwelling there. People in the Pure Land never experience pain, desire, or human suffering. Amida's kingdom has a lotus pond, ambrosia groves, and trees of jewels. Birds and bells perch on the trees. Buddha and his angels circle in the sky, scattering petals.

The Pure Land movement represents an important Buddhist sect in Japanese history. Among its adherents' many beliefs, it was thought that a devout Buddhist who recited Amida's name at the time of death would enter the Pure Land. Much artwork showing Amida often symbolizes this process. According to this belief, the BODHISATTVAS (or future Buddhas) Avalokita and Mashāthama help believers reach this paradise after their deaths. (See PURE LAND BUDDHISM.)

AMIDAJI, TEMPLE OF This famous TEMPLE was built at Akamagaséki (present-day Shimonoseki) to pacify the ghosts of the drowned emperor and men of the TAIRA clan, who died in a great battle for leadership of Japan during the Japanese feudal age. (See FEUDALISM IN JAPAN.) While the spirits were mostly satisfied by the temple, they continued to haunt the area.

The legend is one of many concerning the clash between the Taira and MINAMOTO clans, an important conflict during the Japanese medieval period.

AM-NO-TANABTA-HIME The Shinto goddess of weavers.

AMUSU-KAMI In SHINTO myths, the gods who live in heaven.

ANAN The Japanese equivalent of Ananda, the Indian Buddhist friend and follower of BUDDHA.

ANCESTORS Many people feel a strong link to their ancestors and preserve this link in various ways. In Japan, as in other Asian cultures, ancestors are venerated with small shrines in homes, ANCESTOR TABLETS, and offerings.

According to ancient Shinto Japanese beliefs, after the dead pass through a suitable waiting and purification period, they become deities themselves. During this waiting time, the souls of the dead must be "fed" with prayers and symbolic offerings of food or they become GAKI, hungry ghosts wandering the earth. They can cause great misfortune for the living.

The veneration of generations past is motivated by love much more than fear, and ancestors can be prayed to for guidance and assistance. Traditional Japanese homes include small altars where ancestors are honored and remembered.

The veneration of ancestors is an important part of Shinto traditions. Besides its religious aspects, it helps tie society together. Large family clans in Japan share the responsibility and honor of venerating ancestors at local shrines as well as those in the home.

Animals such as rabbits often appear in Japanese folktales and mythology.

ANCESTOR TABLETS Wooden tablets or *IHAI* with the name, birth, and death dates of ancestors. These are kept in the household shrine or in an ancestral hall. The dead can occupy the tablet temporarily to receive an offering.

ANIMALS IN LEGENDS AND MYTHS In general, early Japanese SHINTO myths do not treat animals as gods, although at times different creatures are included in the stories connected with the deities. The most famous example is probably INARI, the god/goddess of rice who can change into a fox. There are, however, a great number of animals in Japanese legends and folktales.

The hare or RABBIT, for example, is the hero of a tale in the *KOJIKI*, a record of Japan's earlier "history" and of many important myths and ancient beliefs. In the story, he tricks a group of crocodiles into helping him across to the mainland from Oki. The hare lost his fur in the process but was helped by OKUNINUSHI, a young man who used pollen to restore his white hair. The grateful rabbit then helped Okuninushi win the hand of a princess.

In another tale, a rabbit helps avenge the death of an old woman by tricking a wily BADGER. Badgers often appear as evil or malicious beings, along with CATS and FOXES.

Dogs, birds, and horses are just some of the other animals that figure in many of the legends. Many of these tales were used by storytellers to illustrate moral points, such as the importance of honoring ancestors or remaining truthful and honest.

ANIMISM The belief that souls inhabit objects. Scholars suggest that this idea is the foundation of all religious thought. The SHINTO idea that each natural object or force in the world has an associated KAMI is a good illustration of the concept of animism.

In ancient Japan, it was believed that by praying to these spirits a person could obtain favors. On the other hand, the spirits could become angry if not treated properly.

ANSHITSU A house occupied by a lone Buddhist MONK. In many Buddhist legends, these houses are occupied by the ghosts of monks who once lived in them. Tales involving *anshitsu*, therefore, are often ghost stories.

ANTOKU (1178–1185) A child emperor during the Japanese medieval period who reigned briefly through regents (1180–1185) at the height of the Japanese feudal period. During this time, the imperial family was involved in a bitter struggle between warring clans. YORITOMO, with his cousin YOSHINAKA, led a force from the MINAMOTO clan against the TAIRA, who controlled the emperor. During a sea battle in April 1185, a member of the royal household took Antoku and plunged with him into the water in the Shimonoseki Straits, drowning the child emperor rather than allowing him to be captured by the opposing forces. The conflict between the clans led to numerous legends and tales.

Antoku's tomb is said to be located in a number of places around western Japan, including the island of Iwo Jima, a result of the spreading of legends about the emperor and the battle.

APOTOPAISM The belief that rituals can prevent disasters or evil. In ancient Japan, for example, offerings were commonly made to the gods at planting time to prevent the crop from being ruined. Some of these rituals continue today.

APIRAHIME The first wife of JIMMU, the legendary first emperor of Japan.

ASHITSU KONOHANASAKUYA's name before she married NINIGI-NO-MIKOTO and bore him children.

ASHUKU-NYORAI The immovable BUDDHA in Japanese Buddhist belief.

ASIAN MYTHOLOGIES Those who study the myths of Japan and other parts of Asia often notice a great number of similarities as they go from country to country. Scholars point out that this has to do with the connected history and prehistory of these places. Often, a story or myth originated in one place then traveled without much change to another. This might happen when people were conquered or invaded. It could also happen during trade or through the efforts of people spreading religion.

Many Japanese myths have parallels in China. This is especially true of legends and myths connected with BUDDHISM. In many cases, these stories actually originated in India, where Buddhism started, before coming to China and Japan.

Besides the stories of China and India, parallels to Japanese myths and legends can be found in the myths of KOREA. This nearby land played an important role in the early history of Japan.

See also CHINESE INFLUENCE; INDIAN INFLUENCE.

ASSEMBLY OF THE GODS According to SHINTO mythology, every year the gods assemble at the holy TEMPLE of IZUMO. There, they consider matters of love for the following year: which humans will fall in love, which loves will be fulfilled, which will be disappointed.

ASURAS In Hindu and Indian mythology, the *asuras* are evil giants who fight men and gods. Japanese Buddhist mythology pictures them as demons locked in constant battle with TAISHAKUTEN (the Japanese version of an ancient Indian god, Indra).

ATAGO-GONGEN Atago is honored as a fire god at the SHINTO SHRINE at Mount Atago. In art, he appears as a soldier. Mythologists have traced Atago-Gongen's humanlike appearance to an eighth-century statue of JIZŌ in a Buddhist TEMPLE.

AWABI Demons of the sea near Nanao in Japan, according to early Japanese mythology. They feast on drowning fishermen and guard jewels kept in seashells.

B

BADGER A wild creature that sometimes appears in Japanese folklore as a mischievous being, able to turn itself into different shapes, including that of humans.

In one favorite tale, a badger visits a Buddhist TEMPLE and then tries to hide himself by turning into a teakettle. In this tale, the badger helps the temple priest; badgers in other stories are sometimes evil. One famous Japanese folktale tells of a RABBIT who fights a badger who has tormented a farmer.

See also ANIMALS IN LEGEND AND MYTH.

BAISHU Baishu is the hero of a Japanese legend involving BENTEN, the Buddhist god of love and good fortune.

According to the tale, Baishu found a love poem on paper in a pool of water near a new TEMPLE dedicated to Benten. He fell in love immediately and went to the temple to ask the goddess to help him find the woman who had written it. He was so determined he came every day and on the seventh stayed all night.

As night turned to morning, an old man entered the temple. Then another man, this one quite young, appeared from the front of temple. The young man told the old one that his help was needed to bring about a marriage. The old man took a red rope, tied one end on Baishu, and lit the other from a temple lantern. As he circled the rope in the air, the young lady who had written the poem appeared. The young man told Baishu that this was the person he wanted. Benten had heard his prayers and decided to grant his wish.

Before Baishu could react, all of his visitors vanished. The woman was gone. He wondered, had he imagined it all?

Puzzled, Baishu began walking home. As he went, he saw the young woman who had been brought to the temple. He said hello, and she began to walk with him. Baishu said nothing about the meeting in the temple, and neither did the girl. But when they reached his house, the young woman said they had been married by Benten.

Overjoyed, Baishu brought her into the house. They immediately began living as husband and wife. Oddly, no one else in the neighborhood seemed to notice. At times, Baishu thought his new wife was invisible to all others. Even so, he was very happy.

A few months later, Baishu was in KYOTO when he met a servant who said his master wanted to meet him. Baishu followed along to a house he had never seen. There, an older man welcomed him as his future son-in-law. Before Baishu could say anything else, the man told him that he had spread poems around the area near Benten's temple and prayed to Benten for a good marriage for his daughter. Benten had answered his prayers and described a future son-in-law who looked exactly like Baishu.

Then the man opened the door and introduced his daughter—the woman Baishu had been living with.

BAKEMONO Spirits in Japanese myth, legends, and folktales with evil powers, such as witches and demons, though the spirits are not necessarily evil themselves. *Bakemono* include KAPPA, *mono-no-ke*, ONI, TENGU, and Yamanba, or YAMA-UBU.

BAKU In Japanese folk belief, the eater of nightmares or bad dreams, which are caused by evil spirits. Baku has a horse's body, a lion's head, and a tiger's feet. When a sleeper awakes from a bad dream, he or she can ask Baku to "eat" the dream. This will turn it into an omen for good.

BALDNESS Artworks that show Buddhist MONKS, saints, and other deities in myth and legend often show them with shaved or bald heads. This is one way for the artist to symbolize that the person or god

A bamboo cutter or woodcutter finds the Moon-Child in the Japanese folktale. Bamboo cutters in ancient tales often display what today might be called "folk wisdom." *(From Yei Theodora Ozaki,* Japanese Fairy Tales, *1903)*

has reached enlightenment, or NIRVANA, through BUDDHISM. The clean-shaven head is also associated with the wisdom that comes with age.

Buddhist monks shave their heads as symbols of their devotion and humility.

BAMBOO CUTTER Bamboo cutters, also known as woodcutters and woodcarvers, are often the heroes in Japanese legends and folktales. By using the bamboo cutter as a character, the storyteller signals that the tale is about ordinary people. A bamboo cutter is a humble person and is often used in Buddhist tales as an ideal everyman.

While the stories cover a wide range of topics and subjects, they show that everyday people can have encounters with gods and the supernatural.

BAMBOO-CUTTER AND THE MOON-CHILD An English title for a popular Japanese folktale, also known as KAGUYAHINE, or "The Shining Princess."

See also BAMBOO CUTTER.

BANZABURŌ A hero of ancient Japanese legend.

According to legend, the mountain gods NIKKŌ and Akagi were fighting. Nikkō was getting the worst of the battles, and so she asked the hero Banzaburō to help her. The huntsman found a giant centipede as he trekked through the forest. He shot out its eye, killing it.

The monster was actually Akagi. As a reward, Nikkō allowed Banzaburō to hunt in all the forests of Japan.

In some legends, Banzaburō is the son of the Monkey King and the Mountain Maid (Yama-hime).

BATO KANNON In Japanese Buddhist mythology, one of the seven forms of KANNON and a manifestation of AMIDA. Bato Kannon helps the poor and looks after the souls of the reincarnated who come to earth as animals.

His Sanskrit equivalent is Hayagriva, the horse-headed Kannon. He is sometimes shown with a horse's head on his hair. He has three eyes and horrible fangs.

BENKEI A swordsman and MONK in Japanese medieval legends.

Benkei was a giant, and in many tales the son of a TENGU, or devil spirit. Large and strong, he was a brilliant fighter—until he encountered the hero YORISUNE (known in most legends as RAIKO).

According to legend, Benkei stood in front of Gojo Bridge in KYOTO, taking swords from any warrior who passed. He planned to build a TEMPLE once he acquired 1,000 swords. He had 999 when Yorisune set out to stop him.

Disguised as a boy playing a flute, Yorisune walked right by Benkei, who hardly even noticed him, until the seemingly weak lad swung around and kicked his battle-ax away.

Benkei lashed out with his sword but missed the youth. Again and again he swung, but he always missed. Finally, he gave up in frustration. Yorisune had beaten him—without even drawing his own sword. Filled with awe as well as fatigue, Benkei asked to follow him. They quickly became inseparable friends.

Benkei fought with Yorisune through many battles against the TAIRA clan, a rival family. Finally, he helped Yorisune win a great victory, vanquishing their rivals at sea despite being outnumbered. But Yorisune's brother YORITOMO, who had always been jealous of him, turned against him. He forced the two heroes to flee. Surrounded by Yoritomo's men, Benkei joined his friend and leader in seppuku, or ritual suicide.

BENTEN (BENZAI, BENZAITEN, BENAI-TEN, DAIBENKUDOKUTEN, MYŌONTEN) The Japanese deity Benten is associated with a wide range of attributes and qualities, and the different stories about her sometimes seem confusing or contradictory. She is seen as a goddess of water, love and wisdom, arts, music, and luck. Her earliest identity may have been as the sister of the god of hell in the Buddhist pantheon. Some sources list her as a SHINTO goddess of good speech and music. But she is best known as a goddess who helps humans gain wealth.

According to one popular myth, Benten once descended to earth to do battle with a dragon who was devouring children. She conquered him in an unusual way: she married him. Occasionally she is seen in art riding on the dragon or a serpent. (See DRAGONS.)

Some scholars believe that Benten was a water god or became associated or confused with a water deity dating from before the spread of Buddhist beliefs. There is a story that the island of Enoshima rose from the water to receive her footsteps, which might support these theories. Others trace her to the Hindu river and deity Saravatī, the wife of Brahamā and the goddess of speech and music.

Artworks sometimes show Benten with eight arms. In her hands she holds a sword, a jewel, a bow, an arrow, a wheel, and a key, which symbolize some of her many attributes or qualities.

Geishas, dancers, and musicians consider her their patron. Gamblers hoping for luck call on her. Benten is one of the SHICHI FUKUJIN, the Seven Gods of Happiness. She is the only female in this group.

BIMBOGAMI In SHINTO mythology, Bimbogami is the god of poverty. Since few people want to be poor, Bimbogami is not generally considered a welcome visitor. Special ceremonies send Bimbogami away, returning good fortune or at least money to the celebrants.

BIMBOMUSHI A wood-boring beetle. The name means "poverty bug." The bimbomushi is seen as an omen or sign of approaching poverty and is related to BIMBOGAMI.

BINZURU-SONJA The Japanese god of cures and fine vision. He himself is in terrible pain, which he cannot escape. Because of his kind nature, he helps others.

In Japanese Buddhist mythology, Binzuru was a RAKAN, or a follower of BUDDHA. He was denied entrance to NIRVANA because he broke his vow of chastity. He dwells on Mount Marishi.

BIRDMEN A name sometimes applied to TENGU.

Tengu are sometimes called "birdmen" because of their wings and claws. (*Richard Huber,* Treasury of Mythological Creatures)

Bishamon guards Buddhists from harm and keeps demons at bay. The woodcut of him dealing with a demon dates from the 19th century. *(Collected by William Anderson in* Japanese Wood Engravings, *1908)*

BISHAMON (BISHAMONTEN) The Japanese god of war and, in some accounts, of wealth or riches. Like a great feudal warlord, Bishamon distributes wealth and protects all who follow the law.

Each of the four COMPASS POINTS is said to have its own guardian. In Japanese Buddhist mythology, Bishamon guards the North. He protects against disease as well as demons.

Bishamon wears armor and holds a spear in his hand. Often he is shown standing on slain demons with a ring or wheel of fire around his head like a halo.

Bishamon is the Japanese version of Vaishravana, one of the GUARDIAN KINGS in Buddhism and the god of war. He is one of the SHICHI FUKUJIN, the gods of happiness and good luck.

Bishamon is also called Tamon or Tamon-ten.

BIWA Lake Biwa, one of the largest lakes in Japan, is the setting for several myths and legends. It is located in west central Honshu, near KYOTO. The depths of the lake are said to be patrolled by a nine-foot-long carp, which devours the bodies of those who drown. It was at Lake Biwa that HIDESATO encountered the DRAGON KING.

BIWA HŌSHI Wandering blind bards or minstrels who entertained at Buddhist TEMPLES and at court with stories and tales drawn from myth and legend.

Biwa hōshi played the *biwa*, a Japanese stringed instrument similar to a lute. In some cases, the minstrels were thought able to drive away unfriendly spirits.

BLUE DRAGON In the Japanese zodiac, the guardian of the eastern signs.

BODHIDHARMA (ca. 440–528) The legendary sage, or wise man, credited with bringing ZEN BUDDHISM to China from India. He is venerated as DARUMA in Japan.

BODHISATTVA In BUDDHISM, someone who has postponed his entry into NIRVANA to serve humankind. A bodhisattva is called a *BOSATSU* in Japan.

BON (OBON) The Festival of Lanterns or the Buddhist Day of the Dead. Bon is sometimes compared to the Christian All Souls' Day. It honors one's ancestors as well as all who have died and is usually celebrated over three days during the summer. (It is held on the 13th to 16th of the seventh lunar month, which works out to July or August.)

A number of practices were traditionally conducted at Bon. Many continue to this day. Large fires—*bon-bi*, or bonfires—were set on mountains or hills to welcome the spirits as they returned from the other world. Paths were cleared from mountains so that ancestors could pass freely. Flowers were set in homes so that the souls could take their form. (A number of flowers are used, including pinks, bellflow-

Lake Biwa in Japan, where Hidesato helped the Dragon King. *(From Isabell L. Bird,* Unbeaten Tracks in Japan, *1880)*

ers, and lilies.) Traditionally, two altars were erected: one for one's ancestors and one for GAKI, hungry ghosts or spirits who have no one to feed them. *Bon-odori,* a special dance to honor the dead, was also performed. SHAMANS who could communicate with the spirits were often present during the festivals to pass messages back and forth.

BOOK OF ANCIENT THINGS   See *KOJIKI.*

BOSATSU *(BUTSATSU)*   The Japanese word for "BODHISATTVA," or Buddha-to-be. In Buddhist mythology, bodhisattvas often have special powers and may behave much like gods in other myths, though they are not technically gods.

A follower of BUDDHISM attempts to achieve ENLIGHTENMENT by renouncing worldly desire and following BUDDHA'S path to enlightenment. When enlightenment is achieved, the devout can enter NIRVANA. However, at this point a devout Buddhist could choose to remain in the world to help others. An enlightened soul who chooses to do this is called a Buddha-to-be because anyone who attains Nirvana is called "Buddha." (The word also is used to refer to the founder of the religion, SIDDHARTHA GAUTAMA.) For many devout believers, this state of helping others represents a great honor on its own.

Since a Buddha-to-be delays entering Nirvana specifically to help others, it is possible to pray to him for assistance. This assistance may take the form of what seem, at least to others, to be magical or even supernatural acts.

In many cases, *bosatsu* were real people who became the subject of legends and tales after their deaths. In other cases, historians have traced the bodhisattvas not to real people but to gods who were added to the Buddhist PANTHEON as the religion spread.

In the West, a rough parallel might be found in some Catholic beliefs about the abilities of saints. Some Catholics pray to saints to intercede for them with God and to grant them some favors or miracles. Like Western saints, an individual *bosatsu* often is considered a patron of certain activities or traits. JIZŌ, for example, guards and helps small children.

BOYS' FESTIVAL   English for TANGO NO SEKKU.

BRIDGE OF HEAVEN   In ancient Japanese myths, the earth is connected to heaven by AMA-NO-UKI-HASHI, a floating bridge between heaven and earth. It is sometimes said to be located near Mount Takachihi, or to have fallen into the sea.

BUDDHA   Buddha means "enlightened one." The word is used in BUDDHISM to refer to either (a) a universal, enlightened soul without beginning or end; (b) a manifestation or aspect of this soul, known in Japan as *nyorai;* or (c) the historical founder of Buddhism, SIDDHĀRTHA GAUTAMA, called SHĀKA in Japan.

In MAHĀYĀNA BUDDHISM, the branch of Buddhism that dominated in early Japan, the historical Buddha is seen as only one of several manifestations or instances of the universal Buddha. Other Buddhas include YAKUSHI, the Buddha of healing; AMIDA, the Buddha of boundless light; and DAINICHI, an all-powerful life force sometimes compared to (or said to be) AMATERASU.

Popularly and especially in the West, the word "Buddha" is often used to refer to the man who started the religion, SHĀKA or Siddhartha Gautama as he was known before attaining ENLIGHTENMENT.

The historical Buddha was born in India around 560 B.C. The following story is told of how he attained enlightenment. While the exact details may or may not be accurate, the story summarizes what many feel is the essence of the individual search for truth that led to one of the world's greatest religions.

A wealthy prince, Siddhartha, had every possible luxury growing up. Yet he became concerned that he was missing something. One day, he left the palace with his servant Channa. They came across a sick man writhing in pain.

"Why does he suffer?" Siddhartha asked.

"Many do," replied the servant. "It is the way of life."

Siddhartha continued on his walk. He found an old man who was suffering great pain.

"Why?" Siddhartha asked.

"He is dying," said the servant. "That, too, is the way of life."

Siddhartha went home and thought about all the suffering he had seen. He decided he must find a solution for his people. He left the palace and went to live with holy hermits. These people believed they could find great spiritual understanding by fasting and denying themselves pleasure. Siddhartha joined them. He fasted and denied himself everything. But when he nearly fainted from hunger, he realized that he could no longer think clearly. He saw finally that this was not the way to understand suffering, let alone solve it. He left the others. After eating to regain his strength, Siddhartha sat under a tree and meditated. At first, he felt and thought nothing but fear and doubts. All night long he meditated. And then in the morning, as the Sun lit the horizon, he found enlightenment. He understood the basic state of humankind and the world. The core of his understanding were the FOUR NOBLE TRUTHS:

- There is much suffering in the world. For example, humans suffer from illness, old age, and death.
- Desire causes suffering. For example, we suffer when we are dying because we desire life.
- Suffering can be ended by ending desire.
- The way to do this is by the EIGHTFOLD PATH: right understanding, right thinking, right speaking, right acting, right occupation, right effort, right mindfulness, and right concentration.

After achieving enlightenment, Siddhartha was named the Awakened [or Enlightened] One, or Buddha. He was called ŚĀKAYUMANI (or Shākayumi) Buddha. *Śākayumi* means "sage of Sakya," the tribe or people Siddhartha belonged to. In Japanese, he is called SHĀKA, Shakuson, or Śākayumi, "the renowned one" or "the world-honored one."

Shāka established monasteries and schools to share his ideas. His talks were recorded and organized as SUTRAS or teachings, after his death. As a religion, Buddhism spread over several hundred years, first throughout India and then to China, Japan, other parts of Asia, and eventually the West.

Tradition holds that Buddha's soul lived many lives before his birth as Siddhartha. Several traditions or legends are connected with his birth. It is said, for example, that his coming was announced by an earthquake. His wife, horse, elephant, and charioteer were all said to be born at the same time.

BUDDHISM One of the world's great religions, Buddhism is based on the teachings of ŚĀKAYUMANI BUDDHA (SHĀKA in Japan), known before ENLIGHTENMENT as SIDDHARTHA GAUTAMA. Buddhism now has many sects, or schools of belief, but in general all Buddhists agree that humans must give up earthly desire and take the EIGHTFOLD PATH to truth in order to reach lasting happiness, or NIRVANA. Buddhists believe that the souls of those who have not achieved enlightenment are reincarnated (born again), repeating the cycle until they can fully understand the nature of existence.

Buddhism began in the sixth century B.C. in India. As it developed and spread, Buddhism was influenced by both new interpretations of its core ideas and the ideas of the culture around it. It reached China in the first century A.D. It spread to KOREA around the fourth century. About the middle of the sixth century, it was introduced to Japan. There it gained popularity during the reign of the Empress Suiko in the seventh century. The religion's important principles are recorded in sutras, which began to be copied in Japan no later than A.D. 673.

During its development, Buddhism separated into two main branches. One, known as THERĀVADA, or "the way of the elders," stayed closer to the literal teachings of Buddha. In general, these sects believed that enlightenment must be earned by individual souls striving on their own.

The other branch, MAHĀYĀNA, saw the earthly Buddha as only one manifestation of a universal soul, or Buddha. Enlightenment could be achieved through the help of others who had already perfected their souls. These were BODHISATTVAS or Buddhas-to-be—BOSATSU in Japanese.

Mahāyāna—or "Greater Vehicle"—more freely adapted and absorbed other religious traditions that it encountered, incorporating local gods and myths into its conception of the universe. In Japan, Mahāyāna Buddhism interacted with SHINTO, the set of ancient beliefs that had been passed down for hundreds of years. As a result, many Shinto gods, myths, and legends gained Buddhist interpretations. The process greatly enriched—and complicated—local myths and legends.

Buddhism also brought new myths and legends to Japan. In some cases, these came directly from Buddhism and Buddhist figures. In other cases, the leg-

Buddhist monks. Some sects believe that enlightenment can only be achieved through the total dedication required of Buddhist clergy. *(From Isabell L. Bird,* Unbeaten Tracks in Japan, *1880)*

ends originated outside of Buddhism but were incorporated in it as it spread.

Many Americans are familiar with ZEN BUDDHISM, an important school of Buddhism that remains popular in Japan. Zen began in India and developed into a prominent sect in China before successfully blossoming in Japan around the start of the 13th century.

The historical Buddha and his early followers lived in India. They communicated in Sanskrit, and that language forms the basis for many Buddhist terms and names to this day.

BUDDHIST DIVINITIES   Unlike an adherent of THERĀVADA BUDDHISM, a person who practices MAHĀYĀNA BUDDHISM may call directly on any of a number of important legendary and mythic figures to help him or her reach ENLIGHTENMENT. The divinities can be grouped into four categories: manifestations of BUDDHA, BODHISATTVAS (known in Japan as *BOSATSU*), Kings of Light, and

GUARDIAN KINGS. Not all sects honor all the divinities equally.

Buddhist divinities, or Buddhas, are the manifestations of the eternal Buddha. Buddhas are thought to appear at regular intervals on earth. There are many; the *BUTSUMYŌE* service features the chanting of the names of 3,000 Buddhas.

The bodhisattvas, or Buddhas-to-be, have delayed entering NIRVANA to help others. A number of these are well known throughout Japan. In many cases, they are based on or confused with older gods, either from India or China.

The "Kings of Light"—in Japan called MYŌ-Ō or Myoo—directly fight evil on behalf of the Buddhas.

The heavenly kings, or deva, are guardian spirits. In Japan, the four heavenly kings who guard the earthly directions are called SHI TENNŌ. Statues of them stand at the temple of Osaku, built for them by Prince Shōtoku (574–622). TAMON-TEN (Tamon) guards the north, ZŌCHŌ-TEN (Zōjōten) the south, KŌMOKU-TEN (Kōmoku) the west, and JIKOKU-TEN the east.

Representations of the benevolent kings, or *ni-ō* (also known as *kongō rikishi*), guard the approaches to some large temples.

Among some of the more important figures in Japanese Buddhism are:

- AMIDA, an important protector of humankind
- DAINICHI, an important Buddha especially venerated in the Tendai and Shingon sects
- FUGEN, the BODHISATTVA or future Buddha of wisdom and understanding
- KANNON, a bodhisattva with several manifestations
- FUDO, a Myō-ō who does battle against avarice, anger, and folly
- JIZŌ, a bodhisattva of great strength
- EMMA-O, the god of hell
- IDA-TEN, who watches over monasteries

BUSHIDO   Developed during the Japanese feudal era (1185–1868), "the way of the warrior," or Bushido, is a set of practices and characteristics that honorable SAMURAI were expected to manifest. It is sometimes compared to feudal chivalry, a code of behavior that was supposed to be followed by European knights during the Western medieval period.

Samurai were swordsmen and soldiers who served *daimyo*, or feudal lords, during medieval times. Unlike the European knights, they were not members of the upper class. According to Bushido, samurai were to be loyal to their lord, brave, highly disciplined, fair, and truthful. While physically strong, the proper samurai also had a sensitive side. He should be able to appreciate the beauty of nature and the arts. While he felt his emotions deeply, he held his sadness inside, since expressing it was a sign of weakness.

BUTSU A Japanese name for BUDDHA, the central figure in BUDDHISM.

BUTSUDAN The small Buddhist ALTAR traditionally kept in Japanese homes to honor ancestors. It is often found with a *KAMIDANA* or "*kami* shelf" for honoring SHINTO *KAMI*. A number of small but important rituals are held at the *butsudan* to honor the dead.

BUTSUDO BUDDHA's path. The Japanese term for BUDDHISM.

BUTSUMYŌE A service observed by devout Buddhists, who chant the names of 3,000 BUDDHAS. The rite is a means of gaining forgiveness for sins.

BUTSUZŌ The statue of BUDDHA or of a member of the Buddhist PANTHEON in a Buddhist TEMPLE. These include some of the most important artworks in Japan, and they are often admired for their own sake.

BUTTERFLY The butterfly is sometimes used as a symbol of the soul in Japanese art. Another insect, the DRAGONFLY, is also used in this manner.

As part of their natural life cycle, butterflies change from one form to another. This serves as a perfect metaphor for Buddhist ideas about the soul and existence. The soul remains constant throughout existence, no matter what form its body takes when reincarnated. Truth may take many forms but its essence—and beauty—remain constant.

Butterflies are also used as general symbols of good luck. Butterfly bows bring good fortune at weddings, for example.

Of course, butterflies are beautiful in and of themselves. There are 265 different species in Japan, and artists delight in recreating their beauty.

C

CALLIGRAPHY   Calligraphy, or the art of hand-writing, was traditionally a highly regarded art form in Japan. In fact, a person who could not make good brush strokes was looked down upon as uncultured. The author of the *TALE OF THE GENJI* criticizes one of her characters' ability at calligraphy to show readers that he is not a good person.

There are five basic scripts. *Tensho* is a stylized form that comes from ancient Chinese and is used for official seals and stamps. *Reisho* is also an ancient script, once used for clerical documents. *Kaisho* is an easily read block style that can now be typeset as well as brushed. *Gyosho* (the word means "running style") can be quickly written, because some characters are linked and others omitted. *Sosho* (grass writing) flows smoothly like a field of grass jostled by the wind; this style can be very artistic, with stretched characters seeming to merge into each other

Some Zen Buddhist monks devote themselves to the calligraphic art, using a special script called *bokuseki* to write minimalist, suggestive poems about the essence of nature and existence.

The beauty of calligraphy is an important part of EMAKI, picture scrolls, which often take mythic and legendary topics as their subjects.

CARP   A symbol of youth, bravery, perseverance, and strength. Scholars have suggested that this association is due to the fish's struggles to swim upstream during mating season.

Carp appear in many legends and folktales, often as monsters. A large carp is said to live in Lake Biwa, living on people who drown there. The lake, one of the largest in Japan, is in west central Honshu, near KYOTO.

In days gone by, some Japanese children heard a folktale about the beginning of the world that had a

Carp symbolize youth and energy in Japanese art and mythology.

giant carp shaking its tail and thrashing the water as it woke beneath the ocean. According to this folktale, the carp's wake created Japan.

CATS   Cats sometimes appear in Japanese legends as evil or malicious creatures. They can change their shapes so that they appear to be human. But not all cats are bad. Even today, the *maneki neko,* or beckoning cat, is a good luck charm that shopkeepers use to help bring customers into stores.

CENTIPEDE   Centipedes are small insects with many legs. They are common all over the world. In Japanese myth and legend, centipedes sometimes appear as horrible monsters. There they are large, powerful beasts that play roughly the same villainous role as fire-breathing DRAGONs in other Asian and Western tales.

One ancient story tells the tale of a monstrously large centipede that lived in the mountains near Lake Biwa. The man-eating monster terrified all who lived nearby, until the DRAGON KING of Lake Biwa called on the hero HIDESATO and asked him to slay it. The hero shot an arrow into the monster's brain and killed it. As a reward, Hidesato received a magical bag of rice. No matter how much rice was taken from the bag, it magically refilled. The bag fed Hidesato's family for centuries.

CHARMS Charms or talismans are often displayed for luck, to bring good fortune, and to ward off evil. In Japan, certain charms called OMAMORI are thought to protect the owner from harm and bring good luck.

CHERRY BLOSSOM The beautiful blossoms of the cherry tree are a universal sign of spring. The blossoms were sometimes used by ancient Japanese artists and writers as symbols of beauty and youth. In Buddhist legends and art, cherry blossoms can be used to remind us of our own imperfection: even something so beautiful as a cherry blossom will soon fall to the ground and wither away.

CHIMATA-NO-KAMI The Shinto god of crossroads.

CHINESE INFLUENCES During much of Japan's early history, China was what we would today call a superpower. Not only was it the dominant country in Asia, but it was the most advanced country in the world. Its influence was felt far beyond its borders.

China's influence was spread throughout Asia in many ways, such as trade, military conquest, diplomacy, and cultural exchanges. In the area of myth and legend, China made an enormous impact on Japan through BUDDHISM, which was probably introduced to Japan first through KOREA, where China also had a major impact. Two other important Chinese philosophies, CONFUCIANISM and TAOISM (also called Daoism), contributed to the store of Japanese legends and myths. China also influenced a broad range of Japanese arts, and it was the Chinese sys-

tem of writing that first allowed Japanese literature to flourish.

CHOYO The annual Japanese Chrysanthemum Festival, held each September 9. The festival celebrates the flower itself, as well as the nation and the emperor, which the CHRYSANTHEMUM can be used to represent in mythological art and literature.

CHRISTIANITY Christianity came to Japan in 1549, when Jesuit priests founded a missionary on Kyūshū with the help of Portuguese traders. Members of the Catholic Church, the Jesuits were dedicated to spreading Catholicism throughout the world. The order also had a reputation for learning, establishing schools throughout the world.

In Japan, the order enjoyed a brief period of influence with the government. Under the leadership of Francis Xavier, members of the order moved to KYOTO and began converting many Japanese. Their conversions eventually included the lord Ōmura Sumita. Sumita ruled the northwestern part of the island of Hizen, and in 1574 he declared that all citizens in his domain would be baptized. Jesuits ran the government of Nagasaki, an important trading port with the West and elsewhere. Somewhere between 150,000 and 300,000 Japanese considered themselves Christians by 1600.

However, persecution began toward the end of the 16th century because the new religion was viewed as a threat to the political power of the military authorities. A number of decrees limiting Jesuit and Christian influence were enforced. In 1597, 26 Christians were crucified in Nagasaki. Years of suppression of Christian influences followed. Japan's policy of shunning foreigners in the 17th century further discouraged the spread of the Western religion. The Catholic community shrank, practicing only in secret. Although Christianity is openly practiced today, it has not had a major influence on Japanese thought or mythology.

CHRYSANTHEMUM A beautiful 16-petal flower, the chrysanthemum is the national flower of Japan. It is the emblem of the emperor and often used to symbolize purity and perfection in art. Some pieces of artwork with mythological themes include chrysanthemums.

CHUJO HIME According to Buddhist myth, KANNON took the human form of Chujo Hime, a historical Japanese nun, and invented the art of embroidery.

Chujo Hime created the Lotus Thread embroidery at the TEMPLE of Toema Dera. The embroidery shows the flowers of Paradise.

CHUP-KAMUI The AINU sun goddess. According to myth, Chup-Kamui was originally the moon goddess. But as she watched over the earth on her very first night, she saw so much sin that she begged the sun god to change places with her.

CLEANSING RITUALS In today's modern societies, people realize they must keep themselves clean in order to avoid certain diseases and illnesses. Many ancient cultures also knew this. They extended the idea to include spiritual cleanliness or "purity" as well as bodily cleanliness.

In ancient Japan, the concept of purity was very important, and it is included in ancient SHINTO myths. In the story of IZANAGI AND IZANAMI, for example, Izanami is unable to return from the underworld because she becomes impure by eating food there. Izanagi does not eat and does escape, but on his return he must purify himself before he can go on.

Izanagi's purification was the first ritual act of cleansing, or *misogi*, an ancient Shinto practice that continues today. The ritual not only purifies the body and soul, it restores the vital, animating force necessary for life. The Izanagi myth shows this, for as the ritual is completed, new gods are formed.

Cleansing rituals are important even outside of TEMPLES and religious practices. Even in America, a visitor to a Japanese restaurant will traditionally be presented with a white washcloth that has been dipped in water. This is not because the waiter sees that his hands are dirty. It is a custom that helps the diner symbolically prepare to eat.

COMPASS DIRECTIONS In Buddhist myth, the four directions of the earth are guarded by the four GUARDIAN KINGS, known as the SHI TENNŌ in Japan. The gods are deva, or HEAVENLY KINGS that predate BUDDHISM and are of Indian origin.

See also INDIAN INFLUENCE.

COMPASS POINTS AND HOUSES CHINESE INFLUENCE brought different ideas about the importance of earthly directions and their influence in people's lives. Feng shui, a Chinese system of organizing buildings according to geographic location, supplied a blueprint for where everything from outhouses to warehouses should be built. Locating parts of a house in certain directions are considered bad luck; for example, a door in the northeast corner of a house will allow evil spirits to enter.

CONFUCIUS (KUNG FU TZE) (ca. 551–479 B.C.) An important Chinese philosopher who set out rules for moral and ethical behavior. He also emphasized respect for history, authority, and tradition. His philosophy and followers influenced China for centuries. The spread of Chinese culture to Japan brought many of his ideas there as well.

One of the most important features of Confucianism is the reverence it holds for tradition and ancestors. The philosophy values social harmony, family loyalty, and continuity from generation to generation. Among other things, these ideas encouraged the writing and keeping of historical records. Confucius did not invent this practice, but he and his followers underlined its importance.

COSMOLOGY A cosmology is a theory of the universe, a kind of map of the way things work. A religious cosmology, for example, would explain where heaven is located.

In the SHINTO cosmology, the sky and earth are connected by a floating bridge, AMA-NO-UKI-HASHI. Gods live in both regions, though the more important gods in the Shinto PANTHEON are generally above. The underworld is called YOMI.

BUDDHISM has many different schools, or sects. In general, however, Japanese Buddhists believe the universe is multilayered, with the top layer inhabited by the formless BUDDHA and the lowest the realm of devils.

CRAB Crabs sometimes appear in Japanese folktales, especially those from areas close to the sea. One favorite and famous tale involves a crab that a young girl saved from becoming a meal.

The story starts with a little girl who buys a crab from a fisherman, saving its life so it can return to its home in the sea. Her father, meanwhile, comes across a frog being eaten by a snake. He tries to free the frog but cannot. Then he makes a fateful offer: if the snake lets go of the frog, he will let it marry his daughter.

To his surprise, the snake lets go. Later that night, a young man knocks on the door. When the father answers, he knows right away that it is the snake in human form. Not sure what else to do, he tells the snake-man to return in a few days. Then with great sorrow he explains to his daughter what has happened, and tells her she has no choice but to marry the snake.

The girl is horrified. She goes to her bedroom and stays there, dreading the future.

A few days later, the snake comes again, though this time in his serpentine form. He ignores the father and bangs on the bedroom door, demanding that his bride come out. Inside, the girl cries in despair. The gods, whom she has always honored with her prayers and devotion, seem to have forgotten her.

But in fact they have not. For there is suddenly a loud noise outside. The door bursts open and a thousand crabs march into the house just as the snake attacks the girl. The crabs destroy the snake, saving the girl who had saved their brother crab.

CREATION MYTH *The Story of Ancient Things,* or *KOJIKI,* recorded around 712, and the *NIHONGI (Chronicles of Japan),* compiled in 720, contain similar material. Together, they are our best records of the Shinto creation myths, the central beliefs of the Japanese people about the earth and humankind's creation.

According to the Shinto creation myth, the world existed as a chaotic collection of gases. Gradually, this matter separated into the earth and sky. Several gods then appeared. These did not have shape or hid their bodies. At the same time, a bud appeared in the floating sea that made up the earth. Two more gods sprang from this shape. Together, these five gods were the sky-KAMI.

Several more gods then appeared, including eight that were mated or in pairs. The last of these were He-Who-Invites and She-Who-Invites, whom we now call IZANAGI AND IZANAMI. This pair of gods were brother and sister as well as husband and wife—companion or complementary gods who belonged together, though they were separate beings.

Izanagi and Izanami discovered that their bodies were different. After performing a ritual around a phallic or fertility symbol, they came together as husband and wife and created a son. This son was malformed, which led them to realize that they had performed their ritual incorrectly. The mistake came in allowing Izanami to speak first. From then on, Izanagi spoke first.

With the ritual done properly, they created eight different islands. These started small but soon grew to the present size, covering the earth. Next, they created a wide variety of *kami,* such as the deity-spirits of the seasons, earth mist, trees, and most other earthly features. But when Izanami gave birth to the FIRE god, disaster struck. Badly burned, she lay down. Several gods were produced from her vomit and waste. Then she died.

Upset, Izanagi killed the fire god, which produced several more *kami.* After much grief, he decided to see his wife, following her to YOMI, which we might call the land of the dead.

When he found her in the palace, Izanami told Izanagi from a distance that she had eaten food there. This, she hinted, would make it difficult for her to return. But she promised to talk to him tomorrow—then disappeared. He promised not to look on her until then—but broke his promise sneaking inside. There he found her body hideously swollen and rotting, surrounded by horrible-looking thunder gods.

Horrified by the corpse, Izanagi fled. Angry, his wife followed. But she could not pass the rock-*kami* he placed between the underworld and the upperworld. Izanami threatened to kill 1,000 men each day. Izanagi said he would create 1,500 to replace them.

Returning home, Izanagi realized that he was impure and had to clean himself. He bathed in a river; many more gods were produced from the sweat of his skin and clothes. As he washed his left eye, the sun goddess AMATERASU was born. From his right eye came the moon god, TSUKIYOMI. Finally from his nose came the brave, swift, and impetuous male god SUSANO-WO.

Izanagi told Amaterasu she should rule the heavens. The moon god was made Amaterasu's husband and coruler. But soon afterward he visited the land of INARI, whose name means "jewel of rice storehouse." (Inari can be seen as both male and female. The word *Inara* is sometimes used to refer to the god as female, but *Inari* is the more common rendering in English.) When the moon god asked for food, Inari gave it to him from her mouth and other bodily openings. To Tsukiyomi, this was an insult. He took out his sword and killed the god. From her body came many other foods, vegetables, and useful creatures. (Other versions of the myth say the antagonists were Susano-Wo and UKEMOCHI.)

Amaterasu was so angry when she heard what her brother had done, she refused to see Tsukiyomi any longer. This is why the sun and moon shine at different times, according to the myth.

Meanwhile, Izanagi told Susano-Wo that he should rule over the netherworld. But the impetuous Susano-Wo was jealous of his sister. He destroyed Amaterasu's rice fields and caused great damage. He also defiled her palace by leaving his waste there. At first, Amaterasu believed that he had not done these things on purpose. But when Susano-Wo tore off the roof of her sacred weaving hall and threw in a horse with its skin torn off, she grew angry. She shut herself in a cave and refused to look at him—or anyone.

This caused great suffering, since without the sun, all was night. Finally all of the gods got together and sent AME-NO-UZUME, the "Sky-Frightening Female," to dance for her. UZUME's dance was so outrageous that the gods laughed. Amaterasu came out to see what the laughter was about and caught her face in a MIRROR the gods had positioned near the cave. Curious, she eased out to see her reflection. Daylight returned to the land. The other gods decided to expel Susano-Wo.

Amaterasu decided to bring order to the earth by sending her son to rule it. But her son did not want the job. In his place, she sent her august and honored grandson, the great land divider or great land master called NINIGI-NO-MIKOTO. Amaterasu gave him the mirror to remind him of her, as well as a great sword, KUSANAGI ("grass mower") and the MAGATAMA, a string of jewels. Her grandson's descendants became the emperors of Japan. These THREE TREASURES would remain in the possession of the emperors forever, symbols not only of their power but of their divine heritage.

CREATION OF JAPAN AND THE WORLD

The KOJIKI (*Story of Ancient Things*) describes the basic SHINTO CREATION MYTH. According to the ancient myths, the universe began as a collection of gases without form. Eventually, the cloud began to separate. The lighter gases rose to the top, the heavier sank to the bottom. These gases laid the foundation for the heaven and earth.

Something appeared in the middle space, like the bud a flower might make as it pokes from the earth at spring. Two gods emerged. They hid. A total of seven pairs of gods were born in the same way until an eighth pair, named IZANAGI AND IZANAMI, were born. They created the earth by dipping a special spear (in some translations, a sword) into the sea and then coming together as a married couple.

CUCUMBER

Cucumbers are members of the gourd family of vegetables. Though they can be round, most are usually long, cylindrical, and green. In art and literature, they are used as symbols of fertility and other things.

In Japanese legends and myth, cucumbers are sometimes associated with special powers. Spirits known as KAPPA are often said to ride them through the sky. Some people in ancient Japan believed that the vegetable had special medicinal powers and could ward off evil committed by a *kappa* and other spirits.

DAIBUTSU (DAIBUTSO) Meaning "great Buddha," this word is used to describe a large statue of a BUDDHA in a TEMPLE or great hall, such as the one in the Great Eastern Temple or Toādai-ji in Nara, Japan.

Popularly, the word is used to describe a gigantic statue of the meditating Buddha located near Kamakura. Made of bronze, the statue was cast in 1252: It is among the most popular pilgrimage sites and tourism destinations in Japan outside of KYOTO and TOKYO.

Daibutso, or the Great Buddha, in Kamakura is so famous—and so large—that it merits myths of its own. *(Library of Congress, Prints & Photographs Division [LC-USZ62-095822])*

The statue is itself the subject of a legend, possibly suggested because of its great size. Shortly after it was made, goes the story, a whale heard people talking about it. The whale was angry—it believed it was the largest thing in the world. So it traveled to Kamakura to see what all the boasting was about.

The whale could not fit inside the temple, so a priest volunteered to measure the creature and the statue. Daibutsu unfolded himself from the platform and came down so the priest could do the job properly.

The priest found the whale a tiny bit bigger. The whale went home satisfied, and the statue returned to its platform, where it sits silently to this day.

DAI-ITOKU MYŌ-Ō One of the Buddhist MYŌ-Ō, or Kings of Light. Dai-itoku has six arms, heads, and legs. He is associated with AMIDA, the BUDDHA of boundless light. In Buddhist myth, the Myō-ō help the Buddhas, usually by combating evil.

DAIKOKU (DAIKOKUTEN) Daikoku is one of the SHICHI FUKUJIN, or the Seven Gods of Happiness (or good luck) in popular Japanese belief. He is considered a bringer of wealth, patron of farmers, and protector of the soil. Daikoku wears the golden sun on his chest and holds a mallet that can grant wishes. A friend of children, he is known as "the Great Black One." A fat and prosperous man, he appears in art with his mallet, bags of rice, and sometimes jewels. EBISU is his son.

Placing Daikoku's picture in a kitchen is said to bring good luck and prosperity, ensuring that there will always be nutritious food to eat. Members of the TENDAI Buddhist sect venerate him as the protector of their monasteries.

While Daikoku is a popular figure, there is some confusion about his origin. Some sources state that

Many believe that Daikoku can bestow wealth on those he favors. *(From Isabell L. Bird,* Unbeaten Tracks in Japan, *1880)*

Daikoku is an ancient SHINTO god added to the Buddhist PANTHEON. Others say he is the Japanese equivalent of the Buddhist god known as Mahākāla in India.

Probably because their names are similar, Daikokuten and the Shinto god Daikoku-Sama—also known as OKUNINUSHI—became what scholar Genichi Kato referred to as "dual gods." Their identities became fused and difficult to separate in stories and the popular imagination. This is one example of the way Buddhist and Shinto myths and legends became intertwined.

DAIKOKU-SAMA   See OKUNINUSHI.

DAINICHI (DAINICHI-NYORAI)   The Japanese equivalent of Mahavairocana or Vairocana, Dainichi is the Buddhist personification of purity and wisdom, the first or original BUDDHA. (This is different from the historical Buddha who started the religion. The sense is more of a first god or all-powerful god force.)

He is sometimes called the "great illuminator" or the primordial or first Buddha, injecting life into others. He is also known as the Great Sun Buddha or the Buddha of Ether.

DAISHI (774–834)   A historic figure, Kōbō Daishi was the Buddhist monk credited with the idea of Shinto with Two Faces, the doctrine which united BUDDHISM with native SHINTO beliefs. This idea, also known as RYŌBU-SHINTO, intertwined some of the basic beliefs and myths of the two great religions.

Kōbō Daishi is actually a posthumous title, given to the monk after he died. He was known as Kūkai during life. Kōbō Daishi's name is also rendered as Dobo Daishi and Kabo Taishi.

After his death, many legends began to be told about the holy man. Some probably date from long before his time but were attached to his name after he became famous. Among his legendary deeds were making chestnut trees flower in winter, carving a massive statue of Jizō in a single night, and banishing sea DRAGONS with magic words.

It is said that Daishi's body waits to be united with MIROKU, the BOSATSU of the future. When Miroku comes, Daishi will rise in perfect health as he was in life.

DAOISM   See TAOISM.

DARUMA   Daruma is the Japanese name for BODHIDHARMA, the Buddhist sage who brought ZEN BUDDHISM to China from India before it developed in Japan. There are many legends about the wise man, who was said to be able to concentrate so fiercely that he once spent nine years meditating.

Today, Daruma dolls are colorful good luck charms that help wishes come true. The dolls have two blank eyes. If a person wishes to ensure that a wish will be granted, one eye is painted. When the wish is granted, the person paints the other eye in gratitude.

DAWN GODDESS   Another name for UZUME.

DEATH In ancient Japan, people considered the connection between the living and the dead to be very strong. A person who died did not cease to exist. Instead, if properly venerated or honored, he became a *KAMI*, joining with the gods of the family ancestors. The *kami* could be called on for assistance and advice. But it was also important not to insult or dishonor ancestors, since this would bring harm to the living.

Buddhist attitudes toward death greatly influenced the early Japanese. In BUDDHISM, death can be seen as merely a stage in the process that leads a soul to become or join with BUDDHA. While painful for those left behind, it is still positive for the soul itself. Many Buddhists, especially those who belong to a sect that follows PURE LAND BUDDHISM, believe that the soul goes to a paradise after death before enlightenment. This positive view of the AFTERLIFE contrasted sharply with the underworld described in early SHINTO myth and may be one reason for Buddhism's popularity in ancient Japan.

Traditional Japanese homes often include a BUTSUDAN, a Buddhist ALTAR for honoring dead relatives. According to most old traditions, the dead remain in the house until the 49th day. At that time, the loved one's name is placed on the shrine.

DEMON OF RASHŌMON A famous folktale from 10th century. In the story, the hero, WATANABE, gets the better of an ONI at the Rashōmon gate.

(THE) DEMON ROAD See GAKIDO.

DEVILS AND DEMONS A wide variety of creatures are capable of evil in Japanese legend and myth. Few actually live in hell. The best known demons are probably ONI, beasts so terrible that they can even cause wars.

DEVIL'S ISLAND Onigashima, the island where MOMOTARO (the Peach Boy) freed imprisoned maidens.

DHARMA In BUDDHISM, dharma represents truth and BUDDHA's teaching. It is a reality beyond the changing world and represents the order that guides the universe and should guide an individual's life.

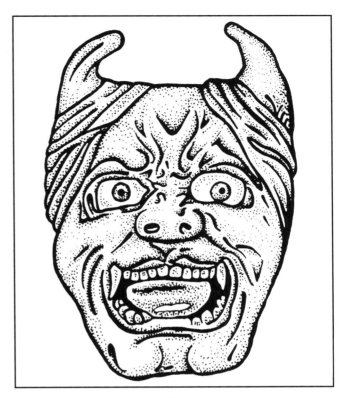

Buddhist demons on the whole are not as potent as Christianity's Satan, but they can still cause sinners great suffering. *(Richard Huber,* Treasury of Mythological Creatures*)*

Demons and devils can take a variety of shapes, at times limited only by the artist's imagination. *(Richard Huber,* Treasury of Mythological Creatures*)*

Legends and tales can be used to illustrate parts of dharma, placing the truth in words or pictures that are easy for all to understand. A teacher might use a story about the SHICHI FUKUJIN, for example, to demonstrate an important quality for a person to have.

DIFFUSION As people and societies change with time, the myths and other stories they tell change as well. This is especially true when the story travels from one place to another. A myth about a certain god or goddess might change as it moves from one place to another. In time, only the outline of the myth might be recognizable.

Scholars studying myths call this process diffusion. They can look at myths that started in one place, such as India, and traveled to another place, such as Japan. When they do, they learn a great deal about both cultures.

There are many examples of diffusion in myths associated with Japanese BUDDHISM, since the religion began in India and eventually traveled to Japan through China and Korea. One such example is the story of BENTEN, which some students of mythology believe is based on tales of Saravatī, the wife of Brahamā and the goddess of speech and music.

DŌJŌ-JI ENGI *Legends of Dōjō-ji*, a famous *enji* (illustrated scroll) in Wakayama, Japan. It dates from the 16th century. The legend in the scroll is set in the 10th century. A MONK from Honshuā came to visit three SHRINES in the region. A married woman fell in love with him and pursued him. The monk ran away, but the woman turned herself into a giant snake and followed. The monk hid inside the bell of the Dōjō TEMPLE. The snake curled around the bell, then breathed fire into it. The monk burned to death.

DŌSHŌ (629–700) According to Japanese Buddhist legend, a holy man who traveled to China and brought back many important teachings, including ZEN BUDDHISM. Dōshō did exist and did travel to China. He was also undoubtedly a wise and devout man. But his visit (653) came much too early for him to have helped found Zen in Japan. Zen's arrival in Japan is generally held to have occurred around A.D. 1200.

DOSOJIN The god of the roads in SHINTO mythology. Dosojin protects travelers.

DOZOKU-SHIN The ancestral KAMI of a *dozoku*, or kinship group. A *dozoku* is a branch of related families connected to a larger line or main family in the same way a thick branch of a tree is connected to the trunk. The ancestral god would be honored by a number of related families.

DRAGON A dragon is a large, mythical beast who seems to appear in stories, legends, and mythical tales in nearly every culture. In Western myths, dragons are almost always up to no good, usually bent on destroying vast pieces of countryside. Japanese dragons are often just as bad, though sometimes they can be good.

Among the oldest dragon tales recorded in Japan is a story of how the Chinese emperor Hwang wished to ride a dragon. He attracted the beast by making a tripod of copper, then climbed on its back and rode through the sky.

A Buddhist TEMPLE located in the province of Mino is called the Dragon Cloud Shrine. According to legend, a dragon appeared there while the temple was being built. In its mouth the dragon carried a pearl, which was believed to carry special powers.

Japanese dragons can sometimes take on other shapes. A number of folk stories feature a dragon that can take the shape of a women—sometimes pretty, sometimes hideous.

What Westerners call dragons are sometimes described in Japanese legends and tales as flying, fire-breathing snakes. In some legends, centipedes

Scholars believe that China influenced the portrayal of dragons in Japanese mythology. *(Richard Huber,* Treasury of Mythological Creatures*)*

act as the evil monsters; they, too, are very similar to dragons.

Chinese lore about dragons may have influenced Japanese tales of the monsters. (See CHINESE INFLUENCE.) In China, the dragon is the beast associated with the east, the direction of sunrise and, in general, positive actions. Early legends and myths about dragons paint them as good spirits. Taoist dragons often help humans. But scholars say the portrayal of dragons turned more negative as BUDDHISM spread through China.

Influenced by the Indian *naga* (dragon), the beasts were more often associated with evil or destruction. As those tales spread to Japan, so did the idea of dragons as demonic monsters.

DRAGONFLY   According to legend, a dead soul can take the shape of a dragonfly, especially during BON, the Buddhist Day of the Dead.

DRAGON KING   Dragon kings appear in a variety of Japanese legends and folktales. Sometimes they are an opponent and obstacle for the hero to overcome. Other times they seek the hero's help. In the story of HIDESATO, for example, the hero rescues the dragon king's kingdom from a centipede.

In Buddhist myth, dragon kings are called RYŪŌ and are considered protectors of Buddha. Ryūō live under the water or are somehow connected with it.

There is no one particular dragon king in Japanese myth.

E

EBISU In Japanese myth, Ebisu is the patron of fishermen and represents the wealth of the sea. He also possesses a number of good qualities, most important honesty, and was used by Buddhist teachers to show the importance of these qualities.

Ebisu was the son of DAIKOKU, the Japanese god of prosperous farming. In works of art he is shown with fish and fishing gear. Historically, his worship was most important in the coastal region near Osaka.

Ebisu and his Father Daikoku are among the SHICHI FUKUJIN, the Seven Gods of Good Fortune.

EDO The former name for TOKYO, the capital of Japan since 1868. (The former capital was KYOTO.) Today the name is sometimes used to capture the historical and cultural spirit of the city.

EIGHTFOLD PATH The things a Buddhist (see BUDDHISM) must do to win release from the cycle of REBIRTH and find NIRVANA. They are expressed in many different ways, but one way of thinking of them is the following:

1. Have the right understanding. To do this, a person must know the FOUR NOBLE TRUTHS.
2. Resolve or think properly. To do this, a person must not be fooled by the illusions of self.
3. Speak properly. To do this, a person must not lie or be frivolous with the truth.
4. Act properly. To do this, a person must not hurt living things, including other people, and must relieve suffering.
5. Have the right work. A person's job must be in keeping with Buddhist teaching; it cannot, for example, violate other steps on the Eightfold Path.

6. Make the right effort. To do this, a person must strive for ENLIGHTENMENT despite obstacles.
7. Keep the right mindfulness. To do this, a person must know the dangers of distracting thoughts and physical states, and avoid them.
8. Have the right concentration. To do this, a person must keep his or her mind free of distractions and be alert to the truth.

EIGHT IMMORTALS In Chinese TAOISM, the Eight Immortals are eight individuals who gained eternal life. Stories about them were used to illustrate the ways a man or woman might achieve ENLIGHTENMENT. These stories often included many magical elements and were highly entertaining as well as instructive. The Eight Immortals are very fond of wine and are sometimes referred to as "The Eight Drunken Immortals."

The eight are Li Tieguai, the first Immortal, whose soul inhabited a beggar's body and later became the patron of pharmacists; He Xiangu, a young woman who could fly and who protected unmarried women; Cao Guojiu, who was the patron of nobility after learning its limits; Han Ziang, who played the flute; Lu Dongbin, the patron of scholars and the guardian of ink makers; Lan Caihe, the patron of the poor; Zhang Guolao, a magician and overseer of happy marriages; and Zhong-Li Quan, the messenger of heaven.

The eight influenced the creation of the Japanese SHICHI FUKUJIN, or Seven Gods of Good Fortune or Happiness.

See also CHINESE INFLUENCE.

EIGHT THUNDERS The terrible beings who chased Izanagi from YOMI after his wife Izanami's death (See IZANAGI AND IZANAMI).

EKIBIOGAMI The SHINTO god of plagues and other epidemic diseases.

EMA Offerings of pictures of a horse made to a Japanese god. Archaeologists believe that the arrival of people who used horses for various purposes, especially warfare, played an important role in shaping early Japanese culture.

EMAKI Painted scrolls of pictures and words that tell stories, often depicting legends, myths, historical events, or a combination of all three. *Emaki* were created primarily during the Japanese middle ages (1185–1868), and the paintings give scholars and historians many hints about life at this time.

The scrolls unfurl horizontally and are meant to be viewed in sections. A scroll is held in both hands, with an open section in the middle. The viewer rolls the scroll with the right hand and unfurls it with the left. Text is meant to be read from right to left. The story is told from different perspectives; some are general overviews, others are more specific and detailed.

Emaki come in all different sizes and lengths; most range from 27 to 36 feet. The *Kibi Daijin Nittoā Ekotoba* measures approximately 72 feet. The number of scrolls in the set could vary like volumes of books; most sets were made up of one to three scrolls.

The art of making these picture scrolls began in China then spread to Japan. The oldest surviving Japanese *emaki* dates from the middle of the eighth century and is a copy of a Chinese hand scroll from the sixth century. The scroll, like many of the period, concerns BUDDHISM.

Japanese artists developed their own styles as well as subjects as they practiced the art. Many scrolls with religious and mythic themes were created during the HEIAN and KAMAKURA PERIODS, from 897 to 1249. Among the most famous from this time are the *Gaki Zōshi*, or *Scroll of the Hungry Ghosts; Jigoku Zōshi*, or *Scroll of Hell; and Shigi-san Engi, Scroll of Legends of Shigi-san Temple*.

Scholars divide *emaki* into several categories. *Monogatari emaki* are like illustrated novels and tell a story with text and pictures. *Nikki emaki* are diaries. A scroll that tells of the origin of a TEMPLE or shrine is called an *engi*.

EMMA-O (EMMA, ENMA) Emma-O is the Japanese Buddhist god of the underworld. He lives in a silver-and-gold castle whose walls are covered with pearls and jewels. Eighteen generals and their armies of soldiers join with numerous demons to guard his kingdom. There are also special guards who have the bodies of men and the heads of horses.

Emma-O decrees punishments and sentences men to different parts of the underworld, where they must pay for their sins. When judging a sinner, he sits on a throne between two heads. A mirror shows all of the dead person's sins, and Emma-O then gives his judgment. There are eight different sections of fiery hell, and eight sections of ice.

Emma-O appears as a bogeyman in many tales. In some stories, Emma-O is very harsh; in others, he is kind and even returns the dead to the land of the living for second chance to live virtuously. JIZŌ, a BOSATSU Buddha-to-be who protects children and pregnant women, often opposes the god, arguing for the souls and usually getting his way. Their battles are a common motif in Japanese artistic scrolls. Other *bosatsu* can also intercede on the dead's behalf.

Emma-O is included in the *Ten Kings Sutra*, an important Buddhist text describing what happens to a soul after death. Different versions of the text exist. Some say 10 kings judge the dead; some say only Emma-O.

The stories of Emma-O and the Chinese god Yanluo are believed by scholars to have come from or been influenced by the Hindu god of death, Yama. (See CHINESE INFLUENCE; INDIAN INFLUENCE.)

EMPERORS According to SHINTO myth, the Japanese emperors descended directly from the goddess AMATERASU, who sent her grandson to earth to rule Japan. According to the early histories, JIMMU TENNŌ, the country's first emperor, descended from these gods. This heritage naturally made the emperor—and all his descendants—divine.

The histories claim that Jimmu ascended to the throne in 660 B.C., almost certainly far too early to be believed. In fact, historians have grave doubts about whether or not the first 10 emperors listed in the ancient Japanese histories existed, though it is possible that these early emperors were based in some way on real people.

Historians point out that the claim of divinity would have added to the early emperor's power and ability to hold sway over the country. It did not, however, guarantee that the emperor was all-powerful, and, in fact, for much of Japan's history, others had more power than the emperor. Even so, the imperial family could never be superseded, and its divinity was not questioned. The status of the emperor in Japanese history has no other parallel in the world.

At the end of World War II (1941–1945), Emperor Hirohito formally declared that the emperor was not a god. The imperial family continues to be held in extremely high regard in Japan, even though its role is now largely ceremonial.

Among the most revered emperors in Japan's very early history is ŌJIN (fl. 200–300, emperor from 270), who was supposedly born after his mother, Empress JINGŌ (fl. 170–269), returned from making war on KOREA. His legendary exploits led him to be identified as the god HACHIMAN in later years. Other important early emperors include KAMMU (737–806, emperor 781–806), who established the capital at KYOTO in 794.

At times, emperors were honored after their deaths because their souls were considered angry or thirsty for revenge. A shrine to Emperor Junnin (733–765, emperor 758–764), for example, was erected after he was exiled and murdered. A number of other emperors were exiled during the difficult middle ages of Japan's history.

Women played an important role as empresses in early Japanese history, and among the country's most storied leaders are several empresses. Empress Jingō, Ōjin's mother, is probably the most famous; her successful campaign against Korea in the third century became an important part of Japanese legend and his-

Until the end of World War II, Japanese emperors, including Hirohito, were considered descendants of the most important gods in the Shinto pantheon. The emperor and his family are still important figures in Japan. *(Library of Congress, Prints & Photographs Division [LC-USZ62-098333])*

tory. Empress Gemmie (661–721, empress 708–714) ordered that the *KOJIKI* be written; the book remains one of the most critical sources of information on ancient Japanese myths and legends available.

ESHIKA Fortune-tellers who use astrology and significant dates to forecast a person's future. Even today, some people will consult an *eshika* about marriage and the best days to hold certain events.

F

FESTIVAL OF LANTERNS Another name for BON.

FESTIVALS A number of festivals with very ancient roots are celebrated in Japan. All have different legends connected with them. In addition to the NEW YEAR FESTIVAL and BON, the occasions popularly known as the Five Festivals are the most popular: Seven Grasses, or NANAKUSA, on January 7; the Girls' Festival, or HINAMATSURI, March 3; the Boys' Festival, or TANGO NO SEKKU, on May 5; the Weaver's Festival, or TANABATA, on July 7; and the Chrysanthemum Festival, or CHOYO, on September 9.

FEUDALISM IN JAPAN As in Europe, Japan's middle ages (1185–1868) featured a societal structure we call feudalism in which lesser vassals owed their allegiance to higher warlords, who maintained their own private armies. In Japan these feudal lords were called *daimyo,* or "great leaders." There were several hundred in the country at the height of middle ages, each controlled a specific area of the country.

The Japanese equivalent of Western knights were called SAMURAI. Like Western knights, they fought with swords and other weapons and armor. Unlike European knights, they were not part of the aristocratic class. The SAMURAI were greatly admired for their bravery, loyalty, and fighting skills. They were the subject of many tales and legends. Their code of behavior, BUSHIDO, was in some ways similar to the Western knights' code of chivalry.

During the latter half of the 12th century, conflict over control of the central government led to a long clash between the TAIRA and MINAMOTO families, which culminated in the GEMPEI WAR (1180–85). Legends and tales from that war later became very popular, helping make samurai romantic figures. A number of colorful legends and folktales, often interwoven with Buddhist themes, were spread after the war.

Japan's internal problems eventually encouraged conflict with China, but when the Mongol (Yuan) Dynasty of China attempted a massive invasion in 1281, a storm, which the Japanese believed to be sent by the divine wind, or KAMIKAZE, helped obliterate the invaders. The gods' role in protecting Japan was immediately celebrated and instilled in history and legend.

Conflict during the early feudal period climaxed in the Onin War. This conflict over selection of the emperor began at the end of the 15th century and embroiled the entire country for roughly the next 100 years. In the end, the war greatly reduced the influence of all but a handful of *daimyo.*

The Japanese government in 1588 adopted a policy of active disarmament called *katanagari,* or "sword hunting." From that point, only samurai could own swords, and the *daimyo* were not allowed to build forts. A period of great peace and prosperity followed. It was during this time that samurai as well as others became more devoted to different arts and literature, and this era saw many great cultural achievements.

The rise of Tokugawa Ieyasu in the early 1600s led to the establishment of the EDO shogunate or military regime and a powerful centralized government. The TOKUGAWA clan would dominate all Japan—and the emperor—for the next two centuries. The decline of their power, exemplified by their inability to prevent the forcible opening of Japan to the West, brought an end to the feudal system.

From a modern perspective, the Japanese middle ages appear to be times of great conflict and war. Certainly there was much bloodshed, but these hundreds of years included many intervals of prosperity, peace, and great artistic achievement as well.

FIRE   As in the West, fire was greatly valued but also feared in ancient Japan. On the one hand it provided warmth and helped prepare nourishing food. On the other hand, there was always a danger it would destroy the wooden structures most Japanese lived in. And during the dry season, strong winds could turn a small house fire into a calamity for an entire village. Thus fire, and the god of fire, KAGUTSUCHI, were well respected throughout Japan. One sign of this respect is the role fire plays in SHINTO ritual.

The fire involved in ritual must be a "pure fire." This must be started in a special way: either by friction with a certain type of wood called *hinoki* (Kiri-Bi fire) or by striking steel against stone (Uchi-bi fire). A fire started in either way can be used at a temple and in ceremonies.

Priests give out the pure fire on New Year's Day at the Temple of Gion in KYOTO. This fire is taken home and then used to light the fireplaces or hearths, where it protects the house for the coming year.

For more on the Japanese fire god, see KAGUTSUCHI and HO-MASUBI.

FIRE GOD   Another name for KAGUTSUCHI.

FIRESHINE AND FIRESHADE   These words are literal English translations of the names of HONOSUSERI and HIKOHOHODEMI, or Honsuri and Hikohoho, the heroes of a popular Japanese mythic tale. Honosuseri is also translated sometimes as "Fire flash" or "Fire glow" and HIKOHOHODEMI as "Fire fade." The exact sense of the words is difficult to describe in English. The names come from the birth sequence: the firstborn, HONOAKARI, had a great deal of the fire quality, the next, Honosuseri, not as much; and the third Hikohohodemi, none at all. Mythologist and translator Post Wheeler suggests that the names correspond to the idea of the sun rising, the sun at noon, and the sun setting.

(THE) FISHER BOY TALE   See URASHIMA TARO.

FLOATING BRIDGE   The Floating Bridge connects heaven and earth in SHINTO myths. (See AMA-NO-UKI-HASHI.)

FORTUNE-TELLERS   See *ESHIKA*.

FOUR NOBLE TRUTHS   The essential beliefs in BUDDHISM. Though they may be phrased slightly differently, these interrelated truths are at the heart of all Buddhist sects and schools:

- There is much suffering in the world. For example, people suffer from illness, old age, and death.
- Desire causes suffering. This leads to REBIRTH of the soul, preventing it from reaching ENLIGHTENMENT.
- Suffering can be ended by ending desire. Thus, we can reach NIRVANA by ending desire.
- Desire can be eliminated by taking the EIGHTFOLD PATH: right understanding, right thinking, right speaking, right acting, right occupation, right effort, right mindfulness, and right concentration.

FOXES   Foxes often figure in Japanese legends. Many are able to become or pose as humans, usually taking the form of a beautiful woman. Most cause harm or lead men into sin. For example, a story in the *KONJAKU* (a 12th-century collection of tales) tells of a man who left his family when he was beguiled by a fox. When he was finally rescued, he had to be restored to his right mind by PURIFICATION RITES, the prayers of a monk, and the magic of ONMYŌ.

Important exceptions include foxes connected with INARI, the god of rice. Inari often takes the shape of a fox. The Japanese word for fox is *kitsune*.

FUDŌ (FUDO-MYŌ-Ō)   Fudō is a Buddhist Vidyaraja, or King of Light. He fights greed, anger, and ignorance. He is considered the most popular of the MYŌ-Ō, or Kings of Light, in Japan.

Fudō's guardianship is often invoked at the start of battles or efforts to deal with disasters. Some call him the Unshakable Spirit or the Immovable One and say that he personifies perseverance. He protects against fires and other disasters.

According to one Japanese legend, Fudō lives at the summit of Mount Okiyama, where his palace is surrounded by a wall of flames. Anyone who dares to look at him on his throne is immediately blinded.

A story in the province of Awa connects Fudō with the miracle cure of a blind man. A young girl named O Ai San prayed at the waterfall near Fudō's shrine at Ohara for 100 days. When she returned home, her father had been cured of blindness.

Artists often portray Fudō as an old man in the midst of flames. He has a sword in his right hand and carries a rope to tie demons with in his left. His skin is yellow, red, or black.

Fudō came to Japanese BUDDHISM through the SHINGON sect. The sect regards Fudō as a manifestation of the Buddha DAINICHI.

FUGEN (FUGEN-BOSATSU)
Fugen is an important BOSATSU (Buddha-to-be), the Japanese version of the Indian BODHISATTVA Samantabhadra. He represents innate wisdom or reason.

Many say Fugen can extend people's lives. Often, legends involving Fugen were used by MONKS to help show how all people, no matter how sinful, possess some good qualities.

Fugen rides on a white elephant or elephants. Some artwork shows him with as many as 20 arms, and his elephant with six tusks.

Legend has it that Fugen appeared to the monk Shoku (910–1007). In the vision, Fugen was a courtesan, a woman trained in the art of love. This story is said to show that wisdom can be anywhere.

FUJIN
The SHINTO god of the wind. When the earth was created, Fujin let the winds out of his bag. The winds whooshed away the mist, filling the space between heaven and earth so the sun could shine.

Artworks show Fujin wearing a leopard skin with his bag of winds on his back. His face is terrifying.

FUJI-SAN (FUJI, FUJIYAMA, FUJI NO YAMA, Mount Fuji)
Fuji-san is a sacred spirit mountain and a powerful symbol of Japan. Like many natural phenomena, the mountain is considered a KAMI, or deity in SHINTO belief.

Though popularly called a mountain, Fuji is really a volcano. It last erupted in 1707, when its ash covered TOKYO. Its white-coned top makes it instantly recognizable. Three different volcanoes make up the mountain, which is believed by scientists to have first formed some 600,000 years ago. The base of the mountain extends 78 miles. Fuji-san is part of the Fuji volcanic zone, which runs from the Mariana Islands up through Honshu.

Fuji-san is included in numerous paintings and other kinds of art. During the 16th and 17th century,

Fuji-san, or Mount Fuji, has been an important inspiration for Japanese artists as well as the rest of the nation since ancient times. This woodcut from a 1608 edition of the *Ise Monogatari* (Tales of Ise) includes the mountain in the background. *(Collected by William Anderson in* Japanese Wood Engravings, *1908)*

Mount Fuji's already important status became the focus of many Japanese patriots and nationalists. Today its picture is instantly recognized as a symbol of the country.

Newspaper stories estimate than 200,000 people hike up Mount Fuji every year. This pilgrimage is considered a special achievement, doing honor to the *kami* of the mountain.

According to a popular version of an old Japanese myth, Mount Fuji was simply a benign mountain after its creation in 286 B.C. Many years later, an old man found a baby on the slopes. He raised the girl, called KAGUYAHINE, as his own. In time, she grew into a great beauty. She was so pretty, in fact, that the emperor himself fell in love with her and married her.

Kaguyahine lived with him for seven years. But at the end of this time, she told her husband that she was not mortal and had to return to heaven. She gave him a mirror that always showed her face, then immediately left for her home in the sky.

Heartbroken, the emperor began to climb Mount Fuji. He wanted to join his wife in heaven, and thought the mountain would take him there. But when he reached the top he failed to find her. His love was so great it burst from his chest as a brilliant fire. The fire lit the volcano. From then on, smoke rose from Mount Fuji's cone.

FUKAOTSU A NIO, one of the spirits that guards TEMPLE gates as well as monasteries.

FUKKO SHINTŌ "Revival Shintō" was part of the movement that sought to return SHINTO to its original ideas and national status before Buddhist and Confucian influences. The idea took hold at the end of the 17th century, when Japan began to isolate itself from all Western influence.

Shinto enjoyed a great revival in the mid-19th century after the start of the Meiji Restoration (1868), which once more made the emperor the actual leader of the Japanese government (see MEIJI EMPEROR). The state funded various religious offices following the revival.

FUKU-KENSAKU KANNON A version of KANNON in Japanese Buddhist mythology.

FUKUROKUJU The Japanese god of wisdom, luck, and longevity. Fukurokuju's forehead is so high his face is nearly the size of the rest of his body. An old, very wise man, he is often accompanied by a turtle and a crow, a crane, or a stag. These animals are often used in Japanese art to symbolize a long life. Fukurokuju is the godfather of JUROJIN, another god of long life and old age.

Fukurokuju is one of the SHICHI FUKUJIN, the seven Japanese gods of good luck. His stories are believed to have started in China, and it is possible that he is based on a real Taoist sage (see TAOISM).

FUKUTOMI See HIDETAKE.

FUNADAMA In SHINTO mythology, Funadama is the boat-spirit or goddess of boats. She protects fishermen and other sailors. Charms such as women's hair, dice, or money are inserted into a ship or boat's mast to invoke the protection of Funadama or symbolize her presence.

FUNADAMA MATSURI A special boat festival held in honor of FUNADAMA. The festival, said to date to the Tokugawa period (1603–1867), recalls the prayers of travelers on the Arakawa or Ara River, who prayed for a safe voyage between Chichibu and EDO. The festival, held on August 15, is a major event in Nagatoro in Saitama Prefecture on the Ara-River.

FUTSU-NUSHI-NO-KAMI A SHINTO god of fire and lightning, later honored as a god of war. Futsu-Nushi-no-Kami was said to be AMATERASU's general.

Fukurokuju's large head is a graphic example of how wise he is. He is one of the Shichi Fukujin, or good luck gods. (*Christopher Dresser,* Japan: Its Architecture, Art, and Art Manufactures, *1882)*

G

GAKI   *Gaki* are, literally, "hungry ghosts." In Buddhist mythology, they are said to wander the world thirsty and hungry because they were greedy during their lifetimes. They may also have become *gaki* because their descendants did not make the proper offerings to them at the family or household ALTARS.

Many Buddhists make a small food offering to *gaki* before beginning their meal.

GAKI-DANA   The altar for hungry ghosts erected during the BON festival.

GAKIDO   The Demon Road. In Japanese Buddhist belief, this is the lowest point a soul can inhabit. Gakido is sometimes compared to Purgatory in Christian COSMOLOGY, though the analogy is not perfect.

When a soul dies, it is led to the underworld. After passing over Sanzu-no-Kawa, the river of the dead, it arrives at Gakido. Here its sins are weighed. It must make up for the bad things it did during life before passing on.

GAKKŌ   The BOSATSU of moonlight, or the splendor of the Moon. Gakkō is seen with NIKKŌ, the bodhisattva of the Sun, in artwork.

GAMA (GAMA-SENNIN)   A SHINTO god of old age. In some legends and tales, Gama-Sennin is a sage who can take the shape of a snake. He knows the secret of immortality. Like a snake that sheds its skin as it grows older, Gama-Sennin sheds his and becomes young. In some legends and artwork, Gama rides a powerful stag and holds a scroll of secret wisdom. He may also be accompanied by a toad.

GAUTAMA, PRINCE SIDDHĀRTHA   See BUDDHA.

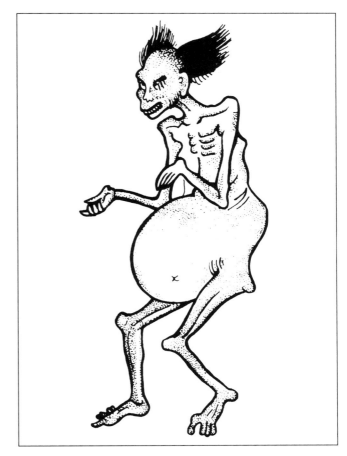

Gaki, or "hungry ghosts," can cause great trouble if not placated or fed. It is customary for Zen Buddhists to offer them rice when they sit down for their own meal. *(Richard Huber,* Treasury of Mythological Creatures*)*

GEKKA-O   The SHINTO god of marriage. Gekka-O's red silk threads bind the feet of lovers.

GEMPEI WAR (1180–1185)   The culmination of a long conflict during the Japanese feudal period for control of the country (see FEUDALISM IN JAPAN).

The TAIRA and MINAMATO clans vied with each other for three decades for control of the leadership of the country. The fight ended in the five-year Gempei War, which the Minamato finally won.

Stories and legends from the war, some more fiction than fact, quickly became popular. The best known is called in English *The Tale of the* HEIKE. Another popular story from the war tells about the hero YORISUNE.

GENJI, TALE OF THE (GENJI MONO-GATARI)
Written by Muraski Shikabu (ca. 973–?1014) in the 11th century, *The Tale of the Genji* provides a vivid picture of Japanese life at the time. This romantic book, called by many the world's first novel, concerns courtly love.

The Tale of the Genji details the exploits of a Genji, the "Shining Prince." The story also tells of his children and descendants. The prince has a variety of wives and mistresses. His love affairs lead to many complications.

Just as today popular books are turned into movies, *The Tale of the Genji* became the subject for a famous *emaki,* or scroll painting, called *Genji Monogatari Emaki,* painted in the 12th century. The book and its stories inspired many other tales and works of art.

Besides its entertainment and literary value, *The Tale of the Genji* provides historians insights into courtly life and Japan during the period.

GIRLS' FESTIVAL   See HINAMATSURI.

GOKURAKU
The term for paradise often used in PURE LAND BUDDHISM.

GONGEN
A Japanese mountain god or an incarnated living spirit. According to Shinto tradition, the mountains of Japan all have deities associated with them. In a way, the gods are the "souls" of the mountains. The most famous is FUJI-SAN, which is a symbol of Japan.

GOOD LUCK
Honoring *KAMI* (Shinto deities) or Buddhist gods was thought to bring good luck in ancient times, and many such practices still exist, including making special rituals and offerings at different SHRINES and TEMPLES. OMAMORI are tokens that can bring good fortune to the holder.

SHOGATSU-MATSURI is an annual festival of renewal and good fortune held January 1–3. During this time, many worshipers visit Shinto shrines to venerate kami and ask for good fortune for the coming year.

The SHICHI FUKUJIN, the Seven Gods of Good Fortune or HAPPINESS in Buddhist tradition, are often seen as symbols of good luck.

GORYŌ (GORYŌ-SHIN)
Evil or unfriendly spirits. Originally, these spirits were the souls of nobles who had died committing evil, such as treason. But it came to be believed that anyone was capable of becoming a *goryō* if they wished to (out of revenge, for example). This change was probably influenced by Buddhist thought.

GOSEKKU
The Five Festivals. These important traditional celebrations relate to ancient religious beliefs as well as myth and legend. The festivals are NANAKUSA, or Seven Grasses; HINAMATSURI, or the Girls' Festival; TANGO NO SEKKU, or Boys' Festival; TANABATA, or Weavers' Festival; and CHOYO, or Chrysanthemum Festival.

GOZANZE-MYŌ-Ō
One of the Japanese Buddhist MYŌ-Ō, or Kings of Light. Gozanze is connected with ASHUKU and is said to live in the East. He has four faces, each with three eyes. The Myō-ō help the BUDDHAS, usually by combating evil.

GOZU-TENNŌ
A Japanese god of the plague, a devastating infectious disease that killed many throughout Europe during the Middle Ages.

GUARDIAN KINGS
Also known as the Shitennō, the four heavenly gods that in Japanese Buddhist myth guard the four compass points. They protect the faithful from harm from each earthly direction. The gods are deva, or heavenly kings, that predate BUDDHISM and were passed along from India (see INDIAN INFLUENCE). Tamon-ten, or BISHAMON, watches the north, ZŌCHŌ-TEN guards the south, KŌMOKU-TEN the west, and JIKOKU-TEN the east.

In some of his tales, the hero RAIKO travels with four companions who are called the Guardian Kings in a reference to these gods. They are WATANABE no Tsuna, Urabe no Suetake, Usui Samitsu, and Kaido-maru or Sakata no Kintoki.

GUNDARI-MYŌ-Ō One of the Buddhist MYŌ-Ō, or Kings of Light, who help the BUDDHAS, usually by combating evil. Gundari is connected with the Buddha Hosho. His body is red; he has fangs; and snakes coil around his hands and legs.

But he is very kind to the poor, giving them heaven's honey.

GREAT LAND DIVIDER (Great Land Master) Names for NINIGI-NO-MIKOTO, AMATERASU's grandson.

GREAT LORD OF THE COUNTRY See OKUNINUSHI.

GUJI The head priest at a SHINTO SHRINE or TEMPLE.

H

HACHIMAN The Japanese god of war, later identified with Emperor OJIN TENNŌ (fl. 200–300), son of Empress JINGŌ.

Perhaps because he was seen as a popular figure, Hachiman was also viewed as a god of peace and a protector of children. He was also worshiped by farmers and fishermen, who asked his help in producing plentiful harvests.

Buddhists identify Hachiman with AMIDA, the BUDDHA of boundless light and with the *BOSATSU* (Buddhas-to-be) KANNON and Daibosatsu. A statue by Kaikei in the 13th century shows Hachiman seated cross-legged with the halo of a Buddhist god or saint behind his head, showing that he is divine.

HAIKU (HAIKAI) Haiku are Japanese lyric poems written in exactly 17 syllables, with a set pattern of five, seven, and five syllables. Traditionally, haiku deal with a season of the year and take their main images from nature. Haiku often contain allusions to Shinto or Buddhist traditions.

At one time, haiku, or "haikai," were so popular that they were created at parties and other social events. Each haiku would be another part of a long linked poem. These were sometimes published and illustrated with images. Topics and styles could range widely and were often humorous.

In Japan, the high point of the haiku is considered to be the 17th to 19th centuries, although the poems continue to be written today. Western poets have also been greatly influenced by the form.

Though haiku may be the most familiar type of Japanese poetry known in the West, Japanese literature is far-reaching and extensive. The history books *KOJIKI* and *NIHONGI* include excerpts of very old poems and songs relating to Shinto and folk myths.

HANIYASU-HIKO The SHINTO god of the earth. His wife is HANIYASU-HIME.

HANIYASU-HIME The goddess of the earth. HANIYASU-HIKO is her husband.

HASE-HIME The heroine of a Japanese legend about a modest young girl, demonstrating how purity and devotion to one's true family are rewarded.

Hase-Hime was born to Prince Toyonari and his wife after they prayed to KANNON. Hase-Hime's real mother died when she was five and she was raised by a cruel stepmother. Nevertheless, she remained a devoted child, and became an excellent musician. When she was 12, she was summoned to the imperial palace to play her koto, or harp, for the emperor. Her stepmother was jealous when the girl did well at the performance and tried to poison Hase-Hime but instead killed her own infant son.

When Hase-Hime was 13, terrible floods ravaged the countryside. The emperor asked if she could write a poem to stop the rains. Her poem succeeded and the stepmother grew even more angry. Finally, she ordered a servant to take the girl to the mountains and kill her. Instead, the servant had Hase-Hime hide in a house there and told the stepmother she was dead.

When Hase-Hime's father was told by his wife that his daughter had run away, he searched in the mountains. Eventually he heard a familiar voice reciting the Buddhist scriptures. Father and daughter were reunited. The stepmother fled, and Hase-Hime eventually married a young man who inherited her father's riches.

HASEO A scholar and poet of the HEIAN PERIOD (794–1185). Though a real person, Ki Haseo (Lord

Haseo) is the subject of a legend that is recorded in an EMAKI entitled *Haseo-kyō Zōshi*, or the *Story of Lord Haseo*, dating from the 14th century. His example shows how real people can become the subject of myths or legends that have little to do with them.

According to the legend, Haseo played *sugoroku* (a dice game) with a demon. He won a beautiful girl in the game. The demon warned Haseo not to touch her for 100 days. But Haseo could not help himself. He embraced her. As he did, she turned to water.

Angered, the demon attacked Haseo. He was saved by TENJIN, the Buddhist protector of scholars.

HASU-KO   Hasu-Ko is the heroine of a popular legend about the power of love and the afterlife. As a young woman, she fell so deeply in love with her husband-to-be that she died before they could wed. Her spirit stole the body of her sister, Kei, so she and her fiancé could live together. In the meantime, Kei's body lay in a motionless coma in her parents' home. At the end of a year, Hasu-Ko returned to her parents with her lover. She told her parents that her soul could only have peace if they wed her fiancé to Kei. Her parents agreed. Kei came back to life and agreed to marry. Hasu-Ko faded away.

HAYA-JI (HAYA-TSU-MUJI-NO-KAMI)   The SHINTO god of the whirlwind.

HA-YAMA-TSU-MI   One of the five MOUNTAIN gods in SHINTO myth. Ha-Yama-Tsu-Mi is the KAMI of the lower slopes.

HEARTH GODS   See KAMADO-NO-KAMI.

HEAVEN   In SHINTO belief, heaven is a dwelling place for the gods, though not all gods live there. It is located in the sky and was created when the ether that existed before the world's creation separated into light and heavier gases. (See AMA.)

According to the Shinto CREATION MYTHS, heaven and earth were connected by a floating bridge called AMA-NO-UKI-HASHI. This eventually collapsed, leaving the earth and heaven separated.

In Buddhist mythology, there are several different worlds, each with its own heavens. According to some sects, humans are born into one of the three

sangai (worlds): desire, form, and spirit. These worlds have their own heavens. For example, the World of Desire has six heavens. The fourth is known as Tuşita (or Tosotsuten), and is said to be located on Mount Sumeru, where TAISHAKU has a large palace. This heaven is mentioned in the *Tale of the HEIKE*.

HEAVENLY KINGS   According to some Buddhist sects, the deva, or heavenly kings of Buddhist mythology, help the BUDDHAS and can be called on by the faithful for assistance. They predate BUDDHISM and were passed along from India. They include the four GUARDIAN KINGS.

HEAVENLY PILLAR   According to SHINTO CREATION MYTH and related legends, the heavenly pillar was formed on the island of Onokoro after IZANAGI AND IZANAMI plunged their magic spear into the land. When they decided to come together as husband and wife, they circled around the spear as part of their courtship. After the ceremony was properly completed, Izanami was able to give birth to other gods.

The spear has been interpreted by scholars as a phallic symbol, a reminder of male fertility. Its role in the creation of gods from Izanagi and Izanami's marriage supports this idea. Some Western scholars point out that European cultures had a similar symbol and rituals involving a maypole, a fertile tree said to have special powers.

HEAVENLY TRUTH   An English translation of TENRIKYO, a SHINTO sect.

HEIAN PERIOD   A critical period in Japanese history, covering 794–1185. It begins with the establishment of the capital at KYOTO (Heian, "Capital of Peace and Tranquility," is the former name of the city) by Emperor Kamu in 794.

At the early part of this period, CHINESE INFLUENCE was very strong, particularly the establishment of a centralized government and Chinese ideography in writing. By the end of the ninth century, however, Japanese culture centered more on local influences.

Art and literature flourished. Local legends and myths were the subjects of many of these works. During this time, SHINTO and BUDDHISM flourished, as did legends and myths connected with them. Important literary works such as the TALE OF THE GENJI deal with life at the imperial court during this time.

HEIKE, TALE OF THE (Heike Monogatari) A Japanese war epic written during the 13th century. Based on earlier oral sources that tell of an important conflict in Japanese history, the epic poem tells the story of the Heike (or TAIRA) clan's fall at the hands of the Genji, or MINAMOTO, clan. The conflict ended with a Minamoto victory in the GEMPEI WAR in 1185.

Many different versions of the tale were told by BIWA HŌSHI, blind bards (hōshi) who told legendary and mythic tales, accompanied by a lute (biwa).

HEROES AS BASIS FOR MYTHICAL GODS
Real people are believed to be the basis of several Japanese mythical or legendary heroes. Of course, their qualities have been altered in the tales about them, and in some cases scholars are unsure of the exact attributes of the original person or have questions about their existence.

Among the different early Japanese legendary heroes who are known to be real are JIMMU, popularly regarded as the country's first emperor; Empress JINGŌ, who waged a successful war against the Koreans while said to be pregnant for three years (see KOREA); and OJIN TENNŌ, who was said to be an incarnation of HACHIMAN, the god of war.

Parallels in the West can be seen in the story of King Arthur. The hero of many legends, Arthur seems a fantastic invention, largely because the stories that involve him include magic and descriptions of things that took place long after he is said to have lived. But after many years of study, historians have come to realize that there was a real Arthur whose exploits helped inspire the very first tales told about him. As these stories became popular, others were told. As the legend grew, very little remained in the story of the real Arthur.

In our own time, Americans have seen some hints of this process with our own real heroes such as George Washington. Many stories have sprung up illustrating Washington's qualities as a leader and hero. For example, nearly everyone knows of the story that the young Washington cut down the cherry tree, then admitted to his father that he did so. Even though historians have shown time and time again that the story was made up by an earlier biographer, the tale is still very popular.

HIDARI A sculptor in Japanese legend. Hidari's statues were remarkably lifelike. One day he was inspired by a great lady's beauty. Awestruck, he fashioned a statue of her. The image was so perfect it came to life.

HIDESATO A legendary Japanese hero who killed many monsters in battle. He is also known as Lord Bag of Rice, or Tawara-Toda.

The hero Hidesato focuses his arrow on the giant centipede terrorizing Lake Biwa—and kills it. The illustration is from a Japanese woodcut. Hidesato was also known as Tawara-Toda, or Lord Bag of Rice. (From Yei Theodora Ozaki, Japanese Fairy Tales, 1903)

Hidesato's greatest fight came at LAKE BIWA, where he encountered a large serpent or DRAGON. The dragon lay sleeping across the path, blocking Hidesato's way. Hidesato climbed up one side and down the other, not bothering to pause until he heard a voice call to him. When he turned, the dragon was gone. Instead, he saw a strange man who wore a dragon crown over his red hair.

"I am the DRAGON KING," said the man, who then asked Hidesato to help him. He knew that Hidesato was very brave, since unlike everyone else who had come near he did not run away at the sight of the king's dragon form.

A giant centipede lived nearby inside Mount Mikami. It killed the king's subjects every day. No one was safe.

Hidesato went with the king to his beautiful, luxurious palace, which was beneath the lake. He enjoyed a wonderful meal and began to fall asleep. Suddenly, he was woken by a peal of loud thunder.

"Here," cried the dragon king.

Hidesato ran to a nearby window and saw a massive centipede. The creature was so large it covered nearby Mount Mikami. Its horrible head glowed with its ugliness.

Hidesato steadied his bow and arrow and took aim at the monster. The arrow flew through the air, a perfect shot. But it bounced off the centipede's head harmlessly.

So did a second arrow. The hero was confounded. Never before had his arrows failed. Then he remembered that human saliva could kill monsters. And so he licked his last arrow, and sent it into the beast.

The centipede hissed and collapsed in death. Lightning flashed. A storm raged all night, but in the morning, the monster was gone.

Hidesato was honored with days of parties. The dragon king gave him a bag of RICE, a pot, a roll of silk, and two bells. The bag of rice never ran out. Neither did the silk, which could be made into many clothes. The pot could cook food without being put on a fire.

After his victory, the hero was given a new name, Tawara Toda, which means (roughly) "lord of the endless bag of rice."

Some scholars believe that Hidesato may be based on a historical Japanese figure.

HIDETAKE Hidetake is the hero of a popular folktale involving Dōsojin, the SHINTO god of travelers. The tale is recorded on a famous EMAKI (scroll) entitled *Fukutomi Zōshī*, or *The Story of Fukutomi*. It is one of many folk stories that combine myth with humor.

Hidetake was an old man. One night he had a dream that Dōsojin gave him a small bell. Unsure what the dream meant, he went to an interpreter who predicted that Hidetake would become rich, thanks to a voice that would come from within himself.

The voice turned out to be the sound of his own flatulence. Hidetake learned how to dance to these noises and soon became famous. Nobles gave him gold and other riches for his performances.

Meanwhile, Hidetake's neighbor Fukutomi became jealous of Hidetake's wealth and success. But he hid his envy and managed to convince Hidetake to take him on as a student. Fukutomi poisoned Hidetake with morning-glory seeds, which gave Hidetake diarrhea.

Hidetake's next performance was a disaster, and his career ended with severe beatings.

The theme of jealous neighbors is repeated in several folktales and legends. Among the best known is "THE MAN WHO MADE TREES BLOOM," a folktale with Buddhist elements.

HIDEYOSHI (TOYOTOMI HIDEYOSHI) (1537–1598) Hideyoshi was a historical general who served under the important Japanese lord ODA NOBUNAGA during the 16th-century wars to unify Japan. A commoner, he managed to win his position as Nobunga's successor through skill and became the country's leading feudal lord. Where Nobunga had ruled primarily through the sword, Hideyoshi tended to be more diplomatic and subtle.

Among his many accomplishments was a great "sword hunt." This program made use of Buddhist beliefs to pacify the countryside. As weapons were gathered up around Japan, their owners were told that the swords were to be melted and made into a statue of BUDDHA, helping to ensure future prosperity.

Hideyoshi is regarded as one of the greatest leaders Japan has produced.

HIGASHI HONGAN-JI An important TEMPLE in KYOTO, once Japan's capital city and today the home of more than 2,000 SHRINES. Its wooden roof is the largest in the world.

HIJIRI

A Buddhist holy man who lives as a hermit in the woods, usually at the foot of or on a mountain. Because of his great devotion, he is able to speak with ANIMALS and gains supernatural powers. These powers help him heal the sick, send hungry ghosts to salvation, and banish devils.

Hijiri did exist, though their deeds are legendary.

HIKOHOHODEMI

In SHINTO myth, Hikohohodemi is one of the sons of NINIGI-NO-MIKOTO, AMATERASU's grandson sent to rule the earth. His mother is KONOHANASAKUYA. His brother is HONOSUSERI, and their stories are intertwined. (See HIKOHOHODEMI AND HONOSUSERI.)

Hikohohodemi married TOYOTAMA, the daughter of the sea god, and lived beneath the sea for many years. When Hikohohodemi returned to land with Toyotama, she became pregnant. She warned Hikohohodemi that he must not watch her give birth. He agreed and she went into a hut to have their child. But Hikohohodemi did not keep his promise. He peeked through a crack in the hut, and watched her turn into a sea dragon.

After giving birth, Toyotama returned to the sea. Her sister, Tamayori-Hime, came from the ocean to look after the child. When the boy grew into a man, he married Tamayori-Hime. Their son had two names: Toyo-Mike-Nu and Kamu-Yamato-Iware-Hiko. According to legend, this son became JIMMU TENNŌ, the first emperor of Japan.

Hikohohodemi is also called Hoori-no-Mikoto or simply HOORI. His name is often translated into English as "fire shade" or "fire fade." He is also known as Utsukine, a nickname that means "Japanese snow flower."

Hijiri were holy men who went to the mountains and often had supernatural experiences. This 18th-century woodcut illustrates a story of an encounter between a Buddhist priest and geese. *(Collected by William Anderson in* Japanese Wood Engravings, *1908)*

Hikohohodemi was given special jewels to control the tides, and he used them when he battled his brother.
(From Yei Theodora Ozaki, Japanese Fairy Tales, *1903)*

HIKOHOHODEMI AND HONOSUSERI In SHINTO myth, Hikohohodemi and Honosuseri were sons of NINIGI-NO-MIKOTO, AMATERASU's grandson sent to rule the earth, and KONOHANASAKUYA. Hikohohodemi was a brave and handsome hunter in the mountains, but he longed to trade places with his brother Honosuseri, a fisherman. Honosuseri said no three times, but finally he agreed.

Hikohohodemi fished all day with his brother's special fishhook but did not catch anything. Honosuseri's luck hunting with Hikohohodemi's bow was just as bad.

Honosuseri was not surprised. "I'm a fisherman," he said when he returned and met his brother. "You're a hunter. Let's get back to our proper places."

Hikohohodemi agreed. But then he had to confess that he had lost his brother's fishhook.

Honosuseri was very angry. Nothing Hikohohodemi did could calm him. Hikohohodemi made 500 hooks from his sword, but Honosuseri would not take them. "I want my fishhook," he kept saying.

Hikohohodemi looked for the hook but soon grew discouraged. He dropped to the ground and began crying as the water lapped on his legs at the shoreline. Shiotsuchi-no-kami, the god of the tides, took pity on him. Deciding to help, Shiotsuchi made a small boat and sent him on a tide to the palace of the sea god, Wata-tsumi. (In some tellings, the god's name is Ryujin. In the version included in HOTSUMA-TSUTAE, or *The Book of Heaven,* he is not a deity but Hadezumi, governor of Sowo.)

When he arrived at the palace, Hikohohodemi hid in a sacred cassia tree near a well as Shiotsuchi had told him to do. Soon, a servant came to take water from the well. He asked the girl for a drink. When she gave him the cup of water, he spit a piece of jade into it.

The girl ran back to TOYOTAMA, her mistress. "There is a handsome prince in the tree near the well," she told Toyotama. "He spit this beautiful jewel into my cup but I can't remove it."

Toyotama went to see him and fell in love. She introduced him to her father, who welcomed Hikohohodemi as his son-in-law. The happy couple lived in the palace for three years, until Hikohohodemi began to seem unhappy. At Toyotama's urging, the sea god Watatsumi asked Hikohohodemi what was wrong. Hikohohodemi told the sea god about the hook. Watatsumi commanded all of the fish to look for the hook. Finally it was discovered in the throat of a sea bream.

Watatsumi gave Hikohohodemi the hook and told him how to put a spell on it so his brother would be cursed. He also gave him the TIDE JEWELS: Shiomitsu-Tama, which creates floods, and Shiohuru-Tama, which removes floods.

A large crocodile (some sources say a shark) carried Hikohohodemi back to his home. Hikohohodemi found his brother and presented him with the lost fishhook. But when Honosuseri took it, Hikohohodemi turned and repeated the curse Watatsumi had given him: "May this hook make you forgetful, unlucky, poor, and foolish."

The curse quickly began to work. As Watatsumi predicted, Honosuseri became poor within three years. He decided to go to war against his brother. But it was a foolish decision. Hikohohodemi used Shiomitsu-Tama to destroy his troops. His brother apologized, and Hikohohodemi removed the flood. After that, Honosuseri pledged to protect Hikohohodemi forever. He was as good as his word.

Hikohohodemi's name is also given as Hoori-no-Mikoto or simply Hoori. Honosuseri's name is also given as Hoderi. These versions of the names are often used together.

Hikohohodemi can be translated as "fire shade" and Honosuseri as "fire shine."

Watatsumi's daughter Toyotama is also known as Otohime and Toyo-Tame.

HINAMATSURI   The Girls' Festival, an annual event in Japan. Held each March 3, Hinamatsuri celebrates the contributions of women to the family and nation. Dolls representing the medieval court are displayed in private homes and apartments. The dolls have usually been passed down for many generations. Stories of famous Japanese women are also shared during the festival.

HINOKAGUTSUCHI   Another name for the Japanese god of fire, KAGUTSUCHI.

HIRUKO   A Japanese god of the morning sun. Hiruko also looks over young children, giving them good health.

Some scholars believe that the Hiruko may have been a sun god honored by many Japanese before AMATERASU. In this interpretation, Hiruko's followers were overshadowed when the YAMATO clan, which honored Amaterasu, gained power.

HISA-ME   In SHINTO mythology, the female demons of DEATH who inhabit YOMI, the underworld. The word is sometimes translated into English as "frowning women."

HISTORICAL PERIODS, EARLY   Japan's early history is often divided into major periods by historians. They are:

  7500 B.C.–250 B.C.: Jōmon   The earliest period for which there is comprehensive archaeological data. The name comes from a type of pottery. The myths and legends of this time have not survived.

  250 B.C.–A.D. 250: Yayoi   Named for a place near Tokyo where its ruins were first discovered, this civilization cultivated RICE. It marked a major change from the earlier period. According to the early Japanese histories, the first emperors descended from the gods and ruled prior to this time.

  250–552: Kofun   This period is named for the large tombs known as *kofun* built during this time. Archaeologists have discovered in the tombs models of buildings very similar to SHINTO shrines. It was during this time that the YAMATO clan came to dominate Japan. Important Shinto myths concerning the creation of Japan were being told and spread during this period, which is also known as the Tumulus period. (See KOFUN PERIOD.)

  553–710: Aduka   This is the time of the introduction and spread of BUDDHISM in Japan. The religion added its own PANTHEON of deities and had a large influence on Shinto as well. (See INDIAN INFLUENCE.)

  710–794: Nara-Nagaoka   During this period, the Japanese emperors used Chinese models to organize the central government. Nara, the capital city, was based on a Chinese plan. The *KOJIKI*, the earliest history of Japan and a storehouse of Shinto mythology, was written during this period.

  794–1185: Heian   This period takes its name from the capital city, Heian ("Capital of Peace and Tranquility"). The city, known today as KYOTO, remains filled with Buddhist and Shinto TEMPLES. The HEIAN PERIOD was the high point of classical Japanese.

HODERI   Another name sometimes used for HONOSUSERI. (See HIKOHOHODEMI AND HONOSUSERI.)

HOJI   In Japanese legend, an evil spirit who lives in the death stone on the moor of Nau. Hoji kills any traveler foolish enough to sleep near the stone, which looks like a tall pillar in the middle of the bare plain.

HOKĒN   A name for the sacred sword, AMA-NO-MURAKUMO-NO-TSURUGI, that AMATERASU gave to her grandson when she sent him to rule the earth.

HOKKE   An important Buddhist sect in Japan, also known as the Lotus Sect, which holds that the *LOTUS SUTRA* contains the only important truth.

The sect was founded in the 13th century by the monk Nichiren, who believed that other strands of BUDDHISM had harmed Japan. Among Nichiren's beliefs was that a dying man or woman could send his or her soul to heaven by saying *Namu-myoho-renge-kyo* (roughly, "glory to the majestic law of BUDDHA's *Lotus Sutra*") at the moment of death. The alternative, according to Nichiren, was a fiery hell.

Though persecuted and repressed, Nichiren preached his beliefs relentlessly. He gained considerable standing after he predicted that Japan would be invaded by the Mongols. (The prediction was made in 1260 and 1268; the Mongols invaded in 1274 and 1281.) Many of his followers were SAMURAI.

Historically, the Lotus Sect has been linked with Japanese nationalism and militancy.

HO-MASUBI The "causer of fire"; a SHINTO god of FIRE, who is called on to prevent fire.

HONINIGI Another name for NINIGI-NO-MIKOTO, AMATERASU's grandson in SHINTO myth. Ninigi was sent to rule the earth. His descendant JIMMU-TENNŌ became the first emperor of Japan.

HONOAKARI The eldest son of NINIGI-NO-MIKOTO and KONOHANASAKUYA; brother of HIKO-HOHODEMI AND HONOSUSERI. He was named Honoakari, or "Fire Light," because he had crawled first from the flames of a hut set on fire to test his mother's purity. His nickname was Mumehito, which means "plum blossom." Honoakari ruled in his father's absence and succeeded him in Hotsuma (today the area of Tokai and Kanto).

HONOSUSERI HIKOHOHODEMI's brother, the son of NINIGI-NO-MIKOTO and KONOHANASAKUYA. Honosuseri is a fisherman. He is said to be the ancestor of the Hayato tribe in Kagoshima; members of the tribe guarded the emperor's palace. Another name for Honosuseri is Hoderi. His name is sometimes translated into English as "fire shine." His nickname is Sakuragi, which means "cherry blossom."

See also HIKOHOHODEMI AND HONOSUSERI.

HOORI Another name sometimes used for Hiko-hohodemi.

See also HIKOHOHODEMI AND HONOSUSERI.

HORAIZAN The Japanese name for P'ēng-lai, one of the chief Islands of the Blessed (paradise) in Chinese Taoist folklore (see TAOISM).

Horaizan has three mountains. The Tree of Life grows on Horai, the tallest mountain. The Tree of Life has gold branches and silver roots. Gems grow in place of leaves and fruits. According to the legends, other vegetation on the island, including grass and even moss, contain the secret of long life. Anyone who eats these plants can live forever—though this can be a mixed blessing.

HORSE RIDER THEORY A theory proposed by Egami Namio in 1948 to explain the rise of early Japanese culture during the KOFUN PERIOD. Though highly controversial in Japan, the theory seeks to explain a wide range of archaeological evidence. It also finds parallels in Japanese myth, especially the stories concerning JIMMU-TENNŌ, the first emperor, with information found in other sources.

According to the theory, the people of Japan were subdued by horse-riding invaders from KOREA during the Yamato era. The invaders became the emperors and leaders of Japan and were responsible for the tombs and other artifacts dating to the Kofun period. (See HISTORICAL PERIODS, EARLY.) The exact circumstances of this time are still being studied.

HOSHO NYORI In Japanese Buddhist myth, Hosho Nyorai is the guardian of treasure.

HOSO-NO-KAMI The god responsible for smallpox, a devastating disease. It was thought possible to ward off the disease by treating Hoso-no-Kami with great respect and making offerings to him.

HOTEI The god of happiness and laughter. He is one of the SHICHI FUKUJIN, a collection of seven popular Japanese Buddhist gods originally used for teaching Buddhist principles but popularly believed to bring good fortune.

Depicted as a very fat man with a big belly, Hotei carries a cloth bag. Inside the bag are children and other precious things. (Hotei's name can be literally translated as "cloth bag.") Statues and paintings of Hotei show him as a jolly Buddhist MONK.

While the Shichi Fukujin are used to illustrate Buddhist principles, scholars say Hotei's origins are actually Taoist.

HOTOKE   The spirits of the dead. This term includes BODHISATTVAS and BUDDHAS.

HOTOTOGISU   The Japanese cuckoo. The bird's call, some say, is really the cry of dead souls longing to return to life.

HOTSUMA-TSUTAE (*The Book of Heaven*) An epic poem that tells the story of Japanese deities from the eighth century B.C. to A.D. 300. The authors are given as Kushimikatama, a minister during the reign of Emperor JIMMU (usually regarded as legendary, though probably based on an actual person), and Ohotataneko, who lived during the reign of Emperor Keiko (also regarded as legendary). It was found by Yoshinosuke Matsumoto in 1966.

HOUSE ALTAR   See ALTARS, BUTSUDAN, and KAMIDANA.

IDA-TEN (IDATEN) The Buddhist god of law and monasteries. Ida-Ten protects MONKS and can be called on to preserve their goodness.

Ida-Ten moves faster than any god or human. This ability makes him the subject of an expression in Japan, "to run like Ida-Ten," which means about the same thing as "to run like the wind" in English. The expression refers to a legend concerning BUDDHA's death. As Buddha lay in his coffin, a demon came and stole one of his teeth. Ida-Ten leapt up and pursued him a great distance, finally catching the devil and retrieving the tooth.

Scholars trace Ida-Ten to the Hindu god Skanda, also known as Kārttikeya. Buddhists began honoring him in the seventh century.

IDZUMO In SHINTO mythology, Idzumo was the first part of the earth where life flourished after creation. It is the "central land of the reed plains."

IHAI An ANCESTOR TABLET used for offerings to the dead in Japanese BUDDHISM. At BON and other special occasions, the souls of ancestors can inhabit the tablets to receive offerings. An *ihai* looks like a rectangle with a rounded top. The ancestor's name and the date of his or her birth and death are written on it.

IHA-NAGA According to SHINTO myth, Iha-Naga was the daughter of Oho-Yama, a mountain god. She fell in love with NINIGI-NO-MIKOTO, but Ninigi preferred her sister KO-NO-HANA.

Iha-Naga means "Princess Live-Long."

IKA-ZUCHI-NO-KAMI The seven SHINTO demons who live in YOMI, the underworld. Their shouts are heard during earthquakes and volcanic eruptions.

IKKAKU In Japanese legend, Ikkaku was a Buddhist SENNIN, or hermit, who became a divinity after he died.

According to legend, while he was alive, Ikkaku was a great warrior as well as a holy man. He captured all of the DRAGONS in the countryside, stopping them from terrorizing the people. Unfortunately, his actions also brought a great drought: the dragons were responsible for the rain.

Farmers and others asked Ikkaku to help, beseeching him with loud pleas. But he would not listen; his faith had made him deaf. The ruler of the land decided the dragons had to be freed, so he sent the most beautiful woman he could find to Ikkaku's cave. Ikkaku not only fell in love the moment he saw her but accepted a glass of sake (rice wine).

Accepting these temptations was a great sin for a devout MONK. Ikkaku lost all of his powers and the dragons escaped, bringing rain to the countryside once more.

IKI-RYO The SHINTO spirit of anger and envy. He is a very harmful presence.

IKKYU In Japanese folklore, Ikkyu is a wise Buddhist priest who always seems to get the better of everyone. Whether he is outsmarting a prince or a merchant or a thief, he gives his rewards to the poor.

I. G. Edmonds, an American who collected the stories, notes that Ikkyu is a "trickster" figure and compares him to Brer Rabbit and Reynard the Fox. Like many Japanese tales, the stories make great use of humor and comedy, as well as using BUDDHISM and other religious aspects to illustrate moral points. Ikkyu is said by many to have been a real priest who lived during the Japanese middle ages, though the person described in the stories is clearly more fictional than real.

IMPETUOUS MALE
Another name for SUSANO-WO.

INARA
The female version of INARI.

INARI (INARA)
The ancient Japanese god—or goddess—of rice and fertility. Myths show Inari as both male and female. He is able to take the shape of a fox and uses foxes as his messengers. Inari was married to UKEMOCHI.

Each year Inari comes down from the mountains to the RICE fields. He is said to take the shape of a spider to torment the wicked and teach them how to behave properly.

Inari stocked the land with rice, the sea with fish, and mountains and forests with game. When he entertained the god TSUKIYOMI, the moon god became angry that these gifts had come from Inari's mouth and killed Inari. Plants, cattle, and silkworms sprang from his body. (In some versions of this story, SUSANO-WO is the killer, and in others, Ukemoche is killed.)

Artists show Inari as an old man—or as a woman with long, flowing hair. Inara (the female version of

the god) is honored in a festival each spring when rice cultivation begins. Scholars link Inara to the Indian god Lashmi and Dewi Sri of Java. The Japanese rice god is also sometimes connected to Uga-no-Mitama, the goddess of agriculture.

Many see Inari as a symbol of prosperity and friendship. Fushimi-Inara, Inari's central temple, was built around 700 in KYOTO. The cultivation of rice remains an important part of Japanese society even today, and shrines to Inari are very common.

INDIAN INFLUENCE
Although India and Japan are many miles apart, scholars have shown that some of the figures in Japanese myths and legends either come from India or have parallels in Indian stories. A major reason for this is BUDDHISM, which began in India and then traveled to China before spreading to Japan. The stories told about BUDDHA himself are the most obvious examples of the Indian influence. The cycle of stories about Buddha's earlier lives known as JATAKA, for example, are mostly based on Indian folktales. Some BOSATSU (Buddhas-to-be) in Japanese Buddhist myth have direct parallels to figures in Indian mythology, as do the Buddhas and other heavenly figures.

ISE-JINGU
Located in Ise in east-central Honshur, Ise-Jingu (Ise Shrine) contains the most sacred Mecincte in Japan. There are two shrines at Ise-jingu: The outer shrine, called the Toyuke Daijingu or Geku, honors the RICE goddess. The Naiku, or inner shrine, holds AMATERASU's mirror, which was given to her grandson, traditionally held to be the first emperor of Japan. Fourteen shrines in the area are affiliated with Ise.

Ise-jingu is torn down and rebuilt every 20 years; the new structures are next to the old ones and look exactly like them. The next reconstruction is due in 2013.

Devotion to Amaterasu at Ise dates at least to the first century A.D.

ISORA
The Shinto god of the seashore. According to one set of myths, Empress JINGO asked Isora for help when she planned to invade Korea. Isora went

Inari is seen as a fox in this late 19th-century drawing of a Japanese temple dedicated to him in the northern part of the country. (*Christopher Dresser,* Japan: Its Architecture, Art, and Art Manufactures, *1882)*

to RYUJIN (the god of the sea or, in other versions, the DRAGON KING) and asked for the TIDE JEWELS to control the waters. These jewels helped Jingō defeat the Korean fleet and paved the way for her victory on the Korean mainland.

ISSUNBOSHI A popular hero of Japanese legend, "Little One Inch."

Issunboshi's parents tried and tried but could not have a child. Finally they prayed for a son. They would be happy, they said, for a child as big as their fingers—and that is exactly what the gods gave them.

Though very small, Little One Inch was otherwise a normal person. He worked hard and was very intelligent and brave. When he was 15, he traveled to KYOTO, the capital of ancient Japan and a holy city. He took a RICE bowl and pair of chopsticks and a needle stuck in a piece of bamboo. These were normal items for a traveler to take, but Little One Inch used them in very unusual ways. He put the bowl into a river and climbed into it. Then he used the chopsticks as paddles and made his way to the city. The needle, of course, was the size of a sword to him and protected him from danger.

In Kyoto, Little One Inch found a job with a noble family. Even though he was tiny, he worked hard and his employers liked him a great deal. One day, Little One Inch went to the temple with his lord's daughter. Along the way, two giant ONI, or devils, attacked them. Acting quickly, Little One Inch managed to distract the demons. The girl ran away. But one of the *oni* grabbed Little One Inch and ate him.

In the demon's stomach, Little One Inch took his needle and stabbed him. Then he crawled up the monster's esophagus, slashing and stabbing the whole way. By the time Issunboshi reached the *oni*'s mouth, the demon was only too happy to spit him out.

The other *oni* sprang to help his friend. But Little One Inch jumped onto his nose and began poking out his eyes with his miniature sword. Defeated and humiliated, the demons fled in terror.

After they had left, Little One Inch found a magic MALLET on the ground. When the girl he had saved returned, she helped him pick it up and make a wish as they struck it on the ground.

The wish was granted—Little One Inch instantly grew into full size. Immediately, his companion fell in love with the strong and handsome SAMURAI. When the pair returned home, the girl's father agreed that they could be married.

ISUKE-YORI-HIME In early Japanese myth and legend, Isuke-yori-hime is the most important wife of JIMMU-TENNŌ, Japan's first emperor.

According to the stories, one day her mother found a red arrow in a stream. At night, the arrow turned into a young man, who was actually a SHINTO god named Omononushi. They married, and their daughter was Isuke-yori-hime.

Legend says Isuke-yori-hime and Jimmu had three sons. Jimmu also had a son by a different wife, Apirahime. This son was named Tagishi-mimi. After Jimmu died, Tagishi-mimi tried to do away with Isuke-yori-hime's children, who were meant to be the rightful heirs of Jimmu. Isuke-yori-hime used songs to warn her children of the danger. One son, Take-nunakawa, killed Tagishi-mimi, ensuring that the rightful heirs would rule Japan. Take-nunakawa became Emperor Suisei.

ITSUKUSHIMA SHRINE One of the most famous SHRINES in Japan. Located on Miyajima Island, the Itsukushima shrine looks out on the Akino Miyajim Great Torii, a large ceremonial gateway in the water built to honor the daughters of SUSANO-WO, the storm god.

ITTAN-MOMEN An evil creature in Japanese legend that appears like a white cloth gag. It wraps itself around a man's or woman's face and suffocates him or her. *Momen* means "cotton."

IZANAGI AND IZANAMI According to the SHINTO CREATION MYTH, Izanagi and Izanami were brother and sister and husband and wife. They were the eighth pair of primordial, or first, beings, existing before the world.

When it came time for Izanagi and Izanami to create the earth, they stood on AMA-NO-UKI-HASHI, the FLOATING BRIDGE of heaven. There they plunged a special spear into the ocean. When they drew it back, the water from the spear fell and formed into the first land, which was the island of ONOKORO. They then stuck their spear into the land, forming the HEAVENLY PILLAR.

Later, the two gods realized that their bodies were not the same. Izanami thought that part of her had not been finished. Izanagi thought he had been given too much. They decided to bring these incomplete parts together. Izanagi suggested that when they did so, Izanami would give birth to more islands. She agreed, and they circled the heavenly pillar. "A handsome man," she remarked when they met. And they immediately made love.

Izanami soon became pregnant. Their child, however, was deformed. He was called Hiruko, or "leach child." The couple abandoned him to the sea.

Perhaps, thought the gods, they had come together in the wrong way. They decided that Izanagi should have spoken first as they circled the pillar, not Izanami. They repeated the ceremony, this time with Izanagi talking first.

It worked. Izanami gave birth to the islands of Japan. She also gave birth to gods and goddesses of waterfalls, the wind, trees, and other vegetation. But tragedy followed when she gave birth to KAGUT-SUCHI, the god of fire. His flames burned her so badly she died.

In grief, Izanagi chopped off Kagutsuchi's head. More gods sprang to life from the dead deity. Izanagi's tears brought still other gods to life. But his wife had gone to YOMI, the land of the dead. Izanagi decided he would find her and bring her back.

But when he arrived in the underworld, Izanagi discovered that Izanami had already tasted the food of the dead. She would not and could not return with him and stayed locked behind closed doors. Izanagi would not give up. Finally he charged into the palace where she was. When he lit his comb as a candle, he saw worms crawling through his wife's distorted, rotting corpse. Eight thunder gods lived in her body, next to the maggots. Izanagi flew away in terror.

Angered that he would not stay with her now, Izanami sent thunder gods and demons to bring him back. They sealed the underworld to try to keep him from escaping. Izanagi had his own magic, however,

and was finally able to escape. As he reached the outer limits of hell, he found three PEACHES. He hurled them at the last demons following him; the devils ran away. From that day, peaches have helped humankind.

Izanami made one last attempt to grab her husband and bring him down to the underworld, but Izanagi rolled a giant boulder across the entrance to hell, blocking her in.

"I will kill a thousand people each day," she promised, angry that he had defeated her.

"Then I will create one thousand five hundred," he promised.

Upon his return to the world, Izanagi washed his left eye. This created the sun goddess AMATERASU. When he washed his right eye, the moon god TSUKI-YUMI was born. SUSANO-WO, the god of the seas and storms, was created from his nose. Susano-Wo, jealous because his sister was chosen to rule the earth, soon disobeyed his father and was banished from heaven.

In the story, the two gods discover that, in order to have a child born properly, the man must speak first during courtship. This may tell us something about the courtship customs at the time the myth was created. It may also tell us about the status of women, and refer to a change from a matriarchal society (one ruled by women) to a patriarchal one (ruled by men).

IZUMO An area of Japan said to be ruled by SUSANO-WO's descendants in early Japanese myth. Traditions in Izumo tell of a different creation myth that holds that SUKUNA-BIKONA, not IZANAGI AND IZANAMI, created the earth. A cycle of myths dealing with Susano-Wo says that he ruled here after his dispute with AMATERASU.

An important SHINTO TEMPLE, Izumo-taisha, is located about five miles from Izumo. It is among the best known and most heavily visited SHRINES in the country. Countless shrines dot the rest of the local area. It is said that the Shinto gods gather in Izumo each October, making the month *kannazuki*, "without gods," everywhere but Izumo, where it is *kamiarizuki*, or "the month with gods." (See KANNAZUKI and KAMIARIZUKI.)

IZUMO CYCLE   A group of SHINTO myths set in the IZUMO region (an area of Japan across from the Korean Peninsula).

These myths talk of SUSANO-WO after he was driven from HEAVEN and continue in the reign of OKUNINUSHI. According to the tales, Susano-Wo built a palace at Suga. After killing a fabulous, eight-headed monster, he married an earth spirit's daughter. Their son-in-law Okuninushi ruled Izumo until AMATERASU sent her grandson NINIGI-NO-MIKOTO to bring order to the earth.

J

JADE Jade stones are often used for jewelry, small sculptures, and other works of art. In legends and myths throughout the world, the material is often said to have special powers. It also appears in stories as a symbol of wealth and power.

In Japan and elsewhere in Asia, many people once believed that jade had the power to detect poison—that a jade cup would break if filled with poison. Jade is an important material in many Chinese legends and myths, some of which entered or influenced Japanese mythology.

The *Tu yang tsa pien*, a chronicle written in China during the ninth century, notes that the Chinese emperor received an impressive game board made of jade as a present from Japan. According to the Chinese author, there was an island east of Japan where a lake or jade quarry produced perfect jade chess pieces.

JĀTAKA An ancient collection of about 550 folktales and fables. The name *Jātaka* translates to "Stories of the Buddha's Former Births." All the stories are supposedly based on facts about the Buddha's earlier incarnations and are said to have originated in India. However, scholars believe that most have no direct connection to BUDDHA or BUDDHISM but, instead, are very old tales that gradually were collected. A few are even included in *Aesop's fables*.

The stories are more than just entertainment. They help to illustrate important qualities in Buddha, such as compassion or charity, and explain how his past lives led to ENLIGHTENMENT.

JEALOUS NEIGHBOR See MAN WHO MADE TREES BLOOM, THE.

JIGAMI In Japan, a *jigami* is a land KAMI or village spirit. The *jigami* is usually the founder of the village or town. A shrine to the *jigami* is often located in the corner of a field.

JIGOKU The term for hell in Japanese PURE LAND BUDDHISM. The site of lowest form of existence, Jigoku is located deep within the earth.

JIGOKUDAYU According to Japanese legend, Jigokudayu was a rich and vain woman. One day, she looked into her mirror. Instead of her beautiful face, she saw a horrible skeleton. This made her realize how empty and vain her life was. She dedicated herself to BUDDHISM, following the teachings of ZEN master Ikky Sojun. *Jigokudayu* can be translated as "lady from hell."

JIKININKI Corpse-eating devils in Japanese Buddhist myth. Many *jikininki* are the spirits of greedy people whose appetites for worldly goods kept them from entering the spirit world. For a story involving one, see MUSO KOKUSHI.

JIKOKU-TEN (JIKOGU, JIKOKU, JIKOKUTEN) One of the HEAVENLY KINGS in Japanese Buddhist mythology. Jikoku is the guardian of the east.

JIMMU-TENNŌ (JIMMU-TENNO) In Japanese legend and history, the first emperor of Japan and one of its greatest early heroes. According to legend, Jimmu established the imperial dynasty.

Jimmu's name can be literally translated as "divine warrior," and that is a good description of him. But he received this name only after his death. Previously, he was known as Toyo-Mike-Nu and Kamu-Yamato-Iware-Hiko. He was the son of HIKOHOHODEMI and a descendant of AMATERASU, the sun goddess. Tradition says that he became ruler of Japan in 660 B.C.

According to Jimmu's story in the NIHONGI, a history of Japan written in the eighth century, he was 45 when he began to conquer new lands. Setting out from Kyushu, he moved with a great army and navy. At sea, a giant god who rode a turtle helped him find new lands. With his fleet he visited many harbors and rivers. He was welcomed by the local leaders, who pledged allegiance to him. In some cases, local gods opposed him, but Jimmu was able to conquer them. These early kings and gods became the heads of important families in Japan.

According to the *Nihongi*, Jimmu lost his brother Itsuse after a battle at the Hill of Kusaka. Itsuse died at Mount Kama, where he was buried. (Some scholars studying the ancient histories believe that Itsuse was actually the emperor before Jimmu, and his death brought Jimmu to the throne.) Sad but undaunted, Jimmu continued his conquests. As he crossed into unfamiliar territory in the region of Kumano, a god in the shape of a bear put a spell on him and his army. Poisoned by the spell, every member of the army fell asleep.

One of Jimmu's soldiers dreamed that Amaterasu and a thunder god, TAKE-MIAZUCHI, were talking about Jimmu's troubles. Amaterasu urged Take-miazuchi to go and help Jimmu. Take-miazuchi said there was no need for him to go himself. Instead, he would send the emperor a magic sword, which would slay all of his enemies.

When the soldier awoke from his dream, he hunted for the sword. He found it in a storehouse and took it to Jimmu-Tennō. The sword glittered with light. Jimmu quickly roused his army from their spell and put the rival gods of the region to flight.

Continuing on their journey, the army soon found itself stranded in the mountains. Amaterasu sent a "sun crow" to guide the emperor. The bird was red and had three claws. It led Jimmu down to the area of Uda. Two brothers named Ukeshi governed here. The younger willingly submitted to Jimmu, but the older planned a deadly trap. He built a special hall with a killing machine, planning to lure Jimmu there. But Michi-no-omi, a loyal follower of Jimmu, managed to force the older Ukeshi into the hall instead. After Ukeshi died, Michi-no-omi chopped off his head. Blood flowed thickly.

Eventually, Jimmu led his army to Yamato, an ancient province on Honshu, the main Japanese island. He built his palace-capital at Kasipara. He won over the local countrymen by marrying a beautiful princess named Apirahime. He also took another wife named ISUKE-YORI-HIME, who was descended from a god named Omononushi. It was her children who continued the line of emperors to modern times.

The tales of Jimmu's exploits are legends, and there is considerable doubt about whether he existed at all. The date provided for his rule in the ancient texts (660 B.C.) is considered too early by most experts for an emperor to have ruled a unified Japan.

Still, there must have been a first emperor of Japan. Such a leader would naturally be viewed as a great hero, though the details in stories told about him long after his death may not have been based entirely on fact. Historians believe that the Japanese emperors came from a clan that consolidated power in the fourth to fifth centuries A.D. They are associated with YAMATO, a region in Honshu.

JINGŌ (JINGŪ KŌGŌ, JINGŪ)
In Japanese history and myth, the empress mother of OJIN TENNŌ, who was later identified as the god of war, HACHIMAN.

Empress Jingō (ca. 170–269) made war on KOREA, probably during the fourth century. According to the legend about her, she was pregnant at the time but delayed her son's birth three years until the war was over. Her successful campaign is venerated at the Shrine of Sumiyoshi.

Like many of the stories about Japan's early rulers, the details in the legends about Jingō's life seem fanciful. But the empress herself was probably a historical person.

JINGU
Shrines related to the imperial family. Among the most famous is ISE-JINGU, which contains the MIRROR said to be handed down by AMATERASU to the imperial family.

JINGŪ-JI
A Buddhist TEMPLE built on the grounds of a Shinto SHRINE so that KAMI can be served by Buddhist rituals. The construction of such temples helped unite the two religions.

JINJA A SHINTO shrine. This term does not include the major SHRINES relating to the imperial family, which are termed *jingu*.

JINUSHIGAMI The god of an area. Literally, the "landlord *KAMI*."

JIZŌ (JIZŌ-BOSATSU) One of the most popular *BOSATSU*, or BUDDHAS-to-be, in Japan. Jizō protects children and pregnant women and can argue on behalf of the dead when their sins are judged. Children who die without prayers cannot find their way to heaven, so Jizō comes and takes them there. His power is so strong that he can even protect children in the underworld.

Among other beliefs, Jizō is thought by some to be able to cure toothaches.

Those who devote themselves to him confess their shortcomings during a ceremony called the Confession of Jizō. In art Jizō is shown as a bald man with a pilgrim staff.

Jizō is the Japanese version of the Sanskrit Kşitigarbha, whose name means "womb of the earth."

JŌDO According to PURE LAND BUDDHISM, Jōdo is a paradise ("Pure Land") where souls go after death to await ENLIGHTENMENT.

JŌDO-SHŪ (JODOSHIN) The largest Buddhist sect that followed the teachings of PURE LAND BUDDHISM; also known as the True Pure Land Sect.

JŌMON (JOMON) PERIOD The period of Japanese culture extending from perhaps 7500 B.C. to about 250 B.C.; there is disagreement on when the culture started. The period gets its name from a type of pottery design called *Jōmon* that anthropologists say was common in Japan before the third century B.C. (The designs appear to be the marks of braided rope pressed into the side of the pottery.)

At one time, scientists thought that the people of the Jōmon period were related to the AINU, not modern Japanese. However, recent discoveries have cast doubt on this idea.

Among the artifacts from this prehistoric time are statues of women that may indicate female goddesses. Experts are not sure of the connection between Jōmon beliefs and SHINTO.

JUICHIMEN (JUICHIMEN-KANNON) The Buddhist god of mercy, Juichimen (also Ju-ichimen) Kannon is an incarnation or version of KANNON. He is shown with 11 heads.

JUNTEI KANNON A manifestation of KANNON, the *BOSATSU*, or BUDDHA-to-be, of mercy. He is the Japanese version of the Sanskrit Cundi, the mother goddess Avalokitesuara. This manifestation refers to the Buddha's mother, who nurtures all as a mother nurtures her child.

JUROJIN One of the SHICHI FUKUJIN, Jurojin is the god of old age in Japanese Buddhist mythology. He rides a white stag and is often accompanied by a crane and a tortoise.

Jurojin has a long beard and carries a staff with a book or scroll attached. The wisdom of the world is written in the words of the book. Jurojin enjoys rice wine and is a jolly figure.

In general, old age in Japanese myth and legend is connected with wisdom.

K

KABUKI A highly stylized form of drama developed in Japan roughly from 1603. Kabuki theater is believed to have developed from ancient dance performances that were relatively simple. Today it is a sophisticated and complex art form.

Kabuki has its own conventions and symbols: a special runway or "flower way" (*hanamichi*) to the stage, a prompter or narrator dressed in black, and wooden clappers that provide background music. The acting is very stylized and not realistic. For example, many plays include special sword fights that seem closer to dances than actual battles. Elaborate and beautiful costumes are an important part of the performance.

Some of the best-known Kabuki plays have legendary and historical themes. In *Sukeroku*, for example, a hero named Sukeroku defies a mean SAMURAI. Kabuki has influenced some avant-garde theater in the West.

KAGAMI The Japanese word for MIRROR. The YATA NO KAGAMI is the sacred mirror given by AMATERASU to her grandson when she sent him to rule the world.

KAGURA In SHINTO myth, the dance that the goddess of the dawn, UZUME, performed when she convinced the sun goddess AMATERASU to leave her cave. It is said that this dance is the mother of all dance in Japan. *Kagura* dances are still performed today on special occasions at SHRINES and TEMPLES and form a category of Japanese performing arts.

KAGUTSUCHI (KAGU-ZUCHI) In the SHINTO CREATION MYTH, Kagutsuchi was the god of FIRE born to Izanami. When he was born, Kagutsuchi's fires burned his mother, Izanami, and she died. Kagut-

suchi's father, Izanagi, cut him into eight pieces. Each piece became a mountain. Eight gods sprang from Kagutsuchi's blood.

A ferocious god, Kagutsuchi was greatly feared. He is also known as Ho-Masubi, which means "starter of fire."

In ancient Japan, the danger of fire threatened everyone, even the emperor. Twice a year, ceremonies to honor Kagutsuchi were held at the emperor's palace. The ceremony included the lighting of special fires at the four corners of the building and the recitation of ancient incantations to control the god. See FIRE; IZANAGI AND IZANAMI.

KAGUYAHINE (KAGUYA-HIME) Known in English as The Shining Princess or the "Moon Child," Kaguyahine is the heroine of a famous Japanese myth and folktale that has several different variations.

Kaguyahine lived on the Moon with her father, the moon god. But she was a willful child. Disobedient, Kaguyahine was punished and set down to live on earth. There she was cared for by a poor craftsman, a BAMBOO CUTTER. The bamboo cutter treated her as his own and soon was rewarded by becoming very rich.

Five wealthy nobles offered to marry Kaguyahine. She gave each a quest to seek. None was able to accomplish the goals she gave them, and she remained good and chaste, refusing marriage. Kaguyahine even turned down the emperor's proposal.

In the end, she returned to her home on the Moon. There, she put on a coat of feathers so she would no longer remember the earth and feel sadness for leaving.

A version of the story associated with Mount FUJI has Kaguyahine marry the emperor but still return to heaven. According to this version, her husband's grief lit the volcano inside the mountain.

KAMADO-NO-KAMI A hearth god, today often honored as the god of the kitchen range. In olden days, a hearth warmed the home and was where meals were cooked; it was the center of the home. Thus its protector played an important role in every-day life.

KAMAITACHI The "sickle weasel," a potent monster in Japanese legend. Supposedly, these crea-tures are so fast that no one is believed ever to have seen one. They usually work in small packs: One monster knocks a person down, the second slices him with his teeth, and a third heals him.

KAMAKURA PERIOD A period of Japanese history extending from 1185 to 1333 that takes its name from the city of Kamakura, located southwest of present day Tokyo, the seat of the military govern-ment of the time. The high point of Japan's feudal society, this era is often compared to the Middle Ages of Europe. It was during this time that SHOGUNS (military rulers) and their armies of SAMURAI con-trolled Japan. Many legends and tales date from this period. See FEUDALISM IN JAPAN.

KAMI In SHINTO, gods and spirits beyond human understanding; literally, "superior ones." The term *kami* includes natural forces such as the sea and mountains, not only gods personified in myths. It also includes one's ancestors. The word is usually translated as "gods" or "deities" in English, though the concept goes beyond what we usually think of as gods.

TEMPLES and SHRINES throughout Japan honor *kami*. Rituals or holy practices differ at each place, but the rituals and the shrines themselves all help revitalize the *kami*. At times, the deity is carried out of a temple on a MIKOSHI, a portable shrine for a parade.

Kami can be broken into two broad categories or groups: *amusu-kami,* or the gods who live in HEAVEN; and *kunitsu-kami,* the gods who dwell on earth. Another useful way to group *kami* is according to a natural phenomenon they are connected with, such as a volcano or the wind, and those that are ancestors of living people.

Though the *kami* are divine, they are not all equal in power. The myths and legends reveal that they are not all-powerful. They can be defeated by other gods or otherwise fail to get their way.

The KOJIKI, an eighth-century history of Japan, declares there are "eight hundred times ten thousand" *kami;* we might say "millions and millions." There are certainly a countless number, since *kami* are con-nected with every natural phenomenon and every family in Japan. Those listed in the *Kojiki*—generally just by name—total more than 2,500.

KAMIDANA The SHINTO Japanese household ALTAR, used to honor ancestral spirits and other KAMI, or deities, important to the family.

KAMI-KAZE The god of wind. Kami-kaze blew away the Chinese fleet when they tried to attack Japan in 1281. During World War II, this story was used to inspire young Japanese pilots to launch sui-cide attacks on American warships. The pilots flew planes loaded with bombs into ships, including air-craft carriers. Since that time, similar tactics have been labeled *kamikaze* attacks.

KAMI-MUSUBI The mother of SUKUNA-BIKONA, a SHINTO god of healing.

KAMINARI Known as HEAVEN's queen, Kami-nari creates thunder, according to SHINTO mythology.

KAMI-UTA SHINTO songs sung at TEMPLES.

KAMMU (737–806) Emperor Kammu established the city of KYOTO in 794 and is a revered ancestor of Japan. Kammu reined in Buddhist influence over the government but he also encouraged the practice of the religion. He sent the Buddhist monks Saichō (767–822) and Kūkai (774–835) to China to study. The teachings they returned with greatly influenced TENDAI and SHINGON Buddhism. A replica of Kammu's original palace was built in 1894 in Kyoto. Called the Heian Shrine, it is one of the city's many attractions.

KANA The phonetic writing system, or "syllabary," or the syllables (phonetic symbols) themselves, developed in the ninth century from Chinese characters but fashioned for the Japanese language. The *kana* allowed Japanese writers to use their own language to write legends, romantic tales, and other compositions. This greatly encouraged the creation of Japanese literature.

Historians say that people began writing and reading in Japan only around the turn of the fifth century, when Chinese characters were introduced to Japan. Until the *kana* were invented, all writing and reading was done in Chinese.

KANAYAMA-HIKO God of metals in SHINTO myth. He is married to Kanayama-hime.

KANAYAMA-HIME Goddess of metals in SHINTO myth. She is married to Kanayama-hiko.

KANNAZUKI AND KAMIARIZUKI Literally, "the month without gods" and "the month with gods." According to SHINTO myth and local belief, the gods meet every October in the IZUMO area. This leaves Japan without gods—everywhere but in Izumo, where it is Kamiarizuki, "the month with gods."

KANNON (KWANNON) In Japanese Buddhist belief, the *BOSATSU* (future BUDDHA) considered the god or goddess of mercy. Kannon was originally a male god but eventually came to be considered female. Myths and legends therefore sometimes portray Kannon as male, sometimes as female.

According to myth, Kannon was born when a beam of light flashed from the right side of the Buddha Amitabha. She decided to stay on earth as a BODHISATTVA, or "Buddha to be," and help humankind.

Kannon can take 33 different forms. One of these has 11 heads. Another features a horse's head. One of the most common male forms of Kannon in Japan is Senju Kannon, or the Kannon of a Thousand Arms. The palm of each hand has an eye, symbolizing his all-seeing compassion. Bato Kannon is considered a manifestation of AMIDA, one of the five Buddhas of contemplation. His job is to protect the souls of animals.

There are numerous legends connected with the god/goddess and its different versions. Here is one, recorded on a famous scroll originally painted for a TEMPLE or SHRINE dedicated to the thousand-armed Kannon (Senju Kannon) in Wakayama, Japan. The scroll dates from the 13th century.

A rich man's daughter was very sick. As she lay dying, a young boy visited and cured her by saying a Buddhist prayer over her. Overjoyed and grateful, the girl's father tried to give him riches, but he refused. Finally the boy accepted a red skirt and knife from the girl and left.

A year later, the man and his family went to visit the boy on the far-away mountain where he had told them he lived. They found nothing there but a small hut. Unsure whether it was his house or not, they opened the door and saw thousand-armed Kannon. In one of its hands was the red skirt.

Understanding at last that the bodhisattva Kannon had visited them, the family became MONKS and nuns and sought enlightenment.

Kannon is the Japanese version of the Buddhist bodhisattva Avalokiteśvara, known in China as Guayin or Kuan Yin. Shrines are dedicated to each of Kannon's forms. It is considered a great pilgrimage to visit all 33.

KANNUSHI A SHINTO priest. A *kannushi* generally presides over Japanese weddings as well as ritual purifications and other ceremonies. Their PURIFICATION RITES are an important part of the start of many new enterprises, from building a new office building to buying a new car.

KAPPA Evil and aggressive water spirits in Japanese legend.

The *kappa* are known for drowning small children, but no one who travels near the water is safe from their attacks. Fortunately, their turtlelike bodies cannot stay on land for very long. Water gives them strength, and while on land they have some in a cuplike part of their skulls at the top of their head. When they meet someone, they always bow—and lose some strength as the water runs out. The more water that spills away, the weaker they become.

Kappa have long hair and monkey faces; their skin is yellow-green. They stand roughly four feet high and are about the weight of an eight- or nine-year-old child. Some sources say they may once have been monkeys.

Kappa travel on CUCUMBERS that buzz through the air like dragonflies (see DRAGONFLY) on a summer's day. They eat cucumbers and blood. Wise men can sometimes make friends with *kappa*. When they do, the *kappa* will teach them how to mend broken bones.

One legend tells of a *kappa* that had been capturing people by pretending to be a small child. Innocent looking, it begged passers-by to play pull-finger or tug-of-war. When they agreed, the *kappa*'s strength overwhelmed them, and they were dragged into the nearby lake. There the creature killed them and drank their blood.

One day, the *kappa* tried to trick a man on horseback into playing tug-of-war. He got the better of the *kappa* by spurring his horse quickly while holding onto the monster. As the water spilled off, the *kappa* pleaded for mercy. If the man stopped, said the monkey-faced demon, he would teach the man to mend bones.

KARITEIMO (KARITEI-MO)   See KISHIMO-JIN.

KARMA   The idea that individual souls have a certain fate that cannot be escaped. Buddhists believe that actions, good and bad, can affect the soul's fate. Karma cannot be escaped. A soul must pay for its sins, if not in this life then in the next—or the next, or the next. The only way for a Buddhist to escape the endless cycle of REBIRTH is through ENLIGHTEN-MENT, though Buddhist sects disagree on how it may be achieved.

KAWA-NO-KAMI   The SHINTO god of rivers. Local river gods answer to Kawa-no-Kami, just as a captain answers to a general.

KAZE-NO-KAMI   Another name for KAMI-KAZE.

KEGARE   The Japanese word for "polluted" or "unclean." The concept of clean and unclean or pure and impure can be found in several myths and legends and is an important concept in the SHINTO religion. For example, the concept is at the heart of the

story of Izanami's imprisonment in hell. Once she ate the food of Yomi, the underworld, she became polluted and could no longer return to earth. (See IZANAGI AND IZANAMI.)

Many cultures share similar ideas, believing that certain foods should not be eaten or prepared or served together, or that certain rituals must be followed to cleanse the body and soul once they have become polluted. CLEANSING RITUALS and PURIFICA-TION RITES prepare a person for different activities.

KEIKO   Japanese emperor, probably legendary, called the "Great Perfect Ruling Lord" in the *KOJIKI*. According to that ancient history, Keiko had 80 children, almost all of whom were sent to rule provinces around the kingdom. He traveled widely, battling rebels and monstrous SPIDERS. His son, YAMATO-TAKERU, had many more adventures, slaying monsters and eventually being changed into a white bird at death.

KENRŌ-JIJIN (KENRŌ-JI-JIN)   Solid Earth Being; an earth god in Japanese Buddhist mythology. It is customary to offer prayers to Kenrō when a new structure is built.

KICHIJŌTEN   A Buddhist goddess thought to bestow happiness. She is the Japanese equivalent of Mahādevī, a Buddhist goddess who originated in India.

KI HASEO   Another name for HASEO.

KIJO   A mythical ogre in Japanese legend.

KIKU   CHRYSANTHEMUM, the national flower of Japan and a symbol of the country. A 16-petal *kiku* is represented on the chest of the imperial family, and Japanese emperors are said to sit on the Chrysanthemum Throne.

KINTARO   A hero of a series of popular Japanese folktales, often told to or written for children.

Kintaro ("the golden boy") was the son of Princess Yaegiri, but he lived alone in the woods. As a boy, he spent his days talking and playing with the animals, who would wrestle with him. Eventually, he met with a woodcutter who wrestled Kintaro to a draw. The woodcutter revealed that he was a general and offered to take Kintaro to be trained as a SAMURAI under RAIKO, the great lord. (Raiko is also known as Minamoto YORISUNE and is a historical as well as legendary figure.)

Kintaro joined Raiko and his army of heroes in many adventures. Stronger than any man, Kintaro once came face to face with a monstrous SPIDER. Before the spider could kill him with its poison venom, Kintaro picked up a giant tree and squashed him.

KIRIN A unicorn in Japanese folk belief. The kirin punishes the wicked and protects the good.

KISHI-BOJIN A Shinto goddess associated with fertility and childrearing. Kishi-Bojin helps women have children and protects them after they are born.

KISHIJOTEN The goddess of luck and beauty in Japanese mythology. Kishijoten protects geisha, women who entertain men with song and dance.

An artist's rendering of a *kirin,* the Japanese unicorn. (*Richard Huber,* Treasury of Mythological Creatures)

KISHIMO-JIN (KISIMOJIN, KARITEIMO) In Japanese Buddhist mythology, the mother of demons. As evil as evil can be, Kishimo-jin stole little children and ate them. But then BUDDHA met her. He converted her, and she changed her ways completely. Kishimo-jin became a protector of children instead of their enemy.

Kishimo-jin is also known as Kariteimo. In art, she is shown with a baby at her breast. She often holds a pomegranate, a fruit that symbolizes love and fertility.

Kishimo-jin is especially revered by the SHINGON sect, which usually refers to her as Kariteimo.

KITANO TENJIN See TENJIN.

KITSUNE-TSUKI A fox spirit that can invade or possess the bodies of humans, especially women. According to legend, Kitsune-Tsuki can enter a person's body through his or her fingernails or breast. In general, FOXES are evil spirits in Japanese folktales and legends.

KIYO The subject of a Japanese Buddhist legend, a woman who lived near the Hidaka River. She worked in a local teahouse as a waitress. One day, a priest from far away stopped in the teahouse. They fell in love. But the priest, remembering his vows, soon broke off their relationship.

Kiyo was extremely angry. Deciding to get revenge, she went to a temple devoted to KOMPIRA. There, Kompira taught her magic, and she learned how to turn herself into a fire-breathing DRAGON.

In the shape of a dragon, Kiyo flew to the priest's monastery to find him. But the priest saw her coming and hid under a bell. Kiyo was not fooled. She spat fire and melted the bell, killing the priest.

KŌBŌ DAISHI The Buddhist who helped introduce the idea of "Shinto with two faces," or RYŌBU.
See also DAISHI.

KODOMO-NO-INARI A fox spirit.
See also FOXES.

KOFUN PERIOD The period of Japanese history lasting from approximately A.D. 250 to 552; also known as the Burial Mound period or Tumulus period. Anthropologists gave the era this name because of the large burial sites, or *kofun*, where EMPERORS were laid to rest in this HISTORICAL PERIOD. These sites still exist.

Anthropologists believe that by studying the mounds they have traced the expansion of the YAMATO clan from its origins in what is now the Nara Prefecture. Recent research strongly suggests a link between the Yamato clan and KOREA. Many anthropologists believe members of the clan may have originally come from there. (See HORSE RIDER THEORY.)

There has been much speculation about what Japan was like in the Kofun period. Most scholars believe that it was during this period that the Yamato clan unified Japan through conquest and diplomacy. According to Chinese reports from the third century, Japan was divided into 30 kingdoms. All were under the authority of an empress or princess known as a Pimiko, an ancient form of the word *himeko*, or "princess." The princess is said to have remained in a TEMPLE in close contact with the gods. Others served as her emissaries to the people.

No written Japanese account of this society exists, but scholars believe that hints may be found in SHINTO myths and legends, many of which are thought to have originated in the Kofun period. For example, the story of AMATERASU tells of a powerful goddess who sent her grandson to rule the earth. This story may echo or reflect parts of Kofun society, such as the existence of a strong female figure as ultimate ruler. Historians and anthropologists who hope to find links to this time period sometimes study early Japanese stories.

KOJIKI   The *Kojiki*, or *Book of Ancient Things*, was written around A.D. 712 in a combination of Japanese and Chinese characters. Undertaken at the request of Empress Gemmei (661–721, empress 707–714), its author was Ono Yasumaro, who based it on tales by Hiyeda no Are that were recited at court. It includes some of the most important SHINTO myths and legends.

The *Kojiki* tells of the creation of the earth and Japan by IZANAGI AND IZANAMI, AMATERASU's reign, and the descent of Japan's emperors from gods. The book also contains important information about ritu-als used to invoke or pray to KAMI, the sacred spirits that inhabit the world.

Historians believe that it was commissioned by Empress Gemmei as a way of demonstrating the importance of the imperial dynasty. Showing that the emperor was linked to the gods certainly would have reminded anyone who read or heard the story of his or her power.

At times, the tales in the *Kojiki* are contradictory and confusing, even for specialists who study them for many years. Part of the problem is that the author found it difficult to render Japanese concepts in the Chinese syllabary (writing language), which was the only one available at the time. He had to resort to using some of the Chinese characters to sound out Japanese words.

Still, the *Kojiki* stands today as the single most important text of the Shinto religion and early Japan. Many scholars study the *Kojiki* to see what it reveals about society at the time it was written.

KOJIN   The goddess of the kitchen in SHINTO myth. Kojin lives in a nettle tree. Children are sometimes told that they should never throw away old dolls but instead offer them to Kojin by putting them on the roots of an old nettle tree.

KOMA   The hero of a Japanese story with elements of Buddhist, SHINTO, and folk beliefs. The tale illustrates the importance of compassion, an important theme in BUDDHISM.

According to early Japanese legend, Koma and his brother Ōma were hunting one day in the area of Kyushu. They came upon a young woman who seemed weak. She begged for food, saying she had just given birth. Ōma, the older brother, would not help her, because those who have just given birth are considered impure. But Koma took pity on the young woman and gave her his own lunch.

The woman revealed herself as the Divine Mother of the Mountain, Yama-no-Shinbo. Koma had good fortune and wealth the rest of his life.

KŌMOKU-TEN (KŌMOKU, KŌMOKU-TEN) One of the HEAVENLY KINGS and the guardian of the west in Buddhist myth. He protects the faithful from danger in that COMPASS DIRECTION.

KOMORI-UTA Japanese lullabies.

KOMPIRA (KOMPERA) A popular Japanese god, Kompira is the patron of sailors and a god of prosperity and wealth. During the Tokugawa period (1603–1867), sailors believed that they could calm storms by cutting off a piece of their hair and throwing it into the water while saying Kompira's name. A SHRINE to Kompira is located on Shikoku island in the village of Kotohira.

Kompira is the subject of several different Japanese myths. One compares him to Kubera, an Indian god who is lord of demons. Another identifies him as SUSANO-WO, who helps people.

KONAKI JIJI A terrible monster described in Japanese myth. It appears to travelers as a crying baby, bawling helplessly along the road. But when a person stops to pick up the baby, Konaki Jiji turns into its monstrous full size, crushing the person.

KONGO The staff of Koya-no-Myoin, the mountain god of Mount Koya. The staff has three prongs and emits a bright, magical light. A person possessing the staff will have wisdom and insight. Scholars believe Kongo is the Japanese version of the Indian *vajra,* a special jewel belonging to the mountain god Indra.

KONGO-KAI The essence of wisdom in BUDDHISM (known as Vajradhara in Sanskrit).

KONGO-YASHA-MYŌ-Ō One of the Buddhist MYŌ-Ō, or Kings of Light. Kongo is associated with FUDŌ and protects the north. The Myō-ō help the BUDDHAS, usually by combating evil.

KONJAKU MONOGATARI (*KONJAKU MONOGATARI SHU*) A collection of more than 1,000 tales, known in English as *Tales of Times Now Past.* It includes stories related to the historical BUDDHA and BUDDHISM; Chinese mythology and history; and Japanese history, myth, legends, and fables.

Scholars are unsure when it was compiled, though they believe it was around 1120. They are also not sure who the author (or authors) were, though they believe it was probably a Buddhist MONK working at Mount Hiei. (Tradition says it was Minamoto Takakuni, a real person, but scholars are fairly certain he died before it was written.)

Scholars use *Konjaku* to learn about ancient myths, legends, and folktales. They also study the stories to learn about the Japanese medieval age when they were written.

KONOHANASAKUYA The "flower child" or "blossom princess" in SHINTO myth, Konohanasakuya makes flowers bloom. She was married to NINIGI-NO-MIKOTO, AMATERASU's grandson and ruler of the earth.

According to Japanese legend, Konohanasakuya, then named Ashitsu, met Ninigi on the seashore and fell in love with him. Ninigi went to her father, Oho-Yama, and asked permission to marry her. Oho-Yama tried to persuade Ninigi to marry his oldest daughter, Iha-Naga, instead. Ninigi insisted on Ashitsu.

According to some versions of the myth, the older sister and her mother were angry and spread rumors that Ashitsu had slept with another man. Ninigi, angry and doubtful, left his wife. Ashitsu tried to get him to take her back but he refused.

Eventually Ashitsu realized what had happened. Planting a cherry tree sapling, she prayed to the tree that it would demonstrate whether she had been true or not. If her baby was her husband's, she asked, let the tree blossom forth forever. If not, then let the blossoms wither and die. After planting the tree, she returned home.

In the spring, she gave birth to three boys. She sent word to her husband, but he did not come home. In despair, she shut herself and the children in a pit at the base of the woods on Mount Fuji. She set the woods on fire, vowing that the fire should kill them all if they were not her husband's children.

The children and Ashitsu were saved by a DRAGON from nearby Lake Konoshiro. Finally, Ninigi saw the blossoming cherry tree his wife had planted and realized that she had been faithful and pure. He rushed home to her, winning his way back into her heart with a beautiful poem.

The boys were named HONOAKARI, Honosuseri, and Hikohohodemi (see HIKOHOHODEMI AND HONOSUSERI), or "Fire Light," "Fire Shine," and "Fire Shade," names that referred to the flaring of the fire they had escaped from. Ninigi changed Ashitsu's name to Konohanasakuya ("She Who Makes the Cherry Trees Bloom"). Konohanasakuya raised her boys and died as an old woman on Mount Harami. Other versions of the tale end less happily, with Ashitsu moving alone to a hut in the woods and dying after setting fire to it.

Konohanasakuya was identified with SENGEN-SAMA, a goddess on Mount Fuji. She was also identified with Koyasu, a Shinto deity who protected and nurtured children. These links seem to come from a time after the original myth was formulated.

KOREA   Japan and Korea have a long and complicated history of trade, cultural exchange, and, at times, war. One theory advanced by anthropologists and archaeologists (but very unpopular in Japan because of historical conflicts and prejudice) that the YAMATO clan, and thus all of Japan's ancestors, descended from Korean invaders. This theory is called the HORSE RIDER THEORY, and, if true, it could account for a range of evidence associated with the KOFUN PERIOD.

It is believed that BUDDHISM first reached Japan in the fifth and sixth century through Korea, after its introduction there by Chinese teachers and priests.

A Japanese army under Toyotomi Hideyoshi (1536–98) invaded Korea in 1592. A force of 40,000 warriors marched up the peninsula from the area of Pusan, quickly reaching and conquering Seoul. The occupation came to an end in 1598 after Korean forces backed by China repeatedly counterattacked the invaders.

Japan also invaded Korea during the Sino-Japanese War (1894–95). After defeating the Chinese armies there, Japan established close relations with Korea and annexed it in 1910. Korea remained under Japanese control until the end of World War II in 1945.

Korean mythology has animistic gods for many parts of nature and human society, similar to the KAMI (see ANIMISM). Its myths and legends include mountain gods, a DRAGON KING, and of course many heroes. Like those of Japan, later myths and legends in Korea were greatly influenced by China.

KOSHIN   The god of the roads in SHINTO mythology. Offering a straw horse to Koshin is said to ensure a safe journey.

KOSHOHEI   In Japanese Buddhist legend, Koshohei was a young goatherd who found a sacred place in the mountains and decided to stay there and meditate for 40 years. His brother Shokei, who was a MONK, went to search him out. He found a sage who told him where he would find Koshohei. Shokei found his brother in the grotto, surrounded by white stones.

"Brother, where are your goats?" asked Shokei. Koshohei took his herdsman's staff and tapped on a stone. In its place appeared a goat: All of his animals had been turned into stones for safekeeping.

KOTAN UTUNNAI   An AINU epic poem detailing the adventures of POIYAUNPE.

KOYA-NO-MYOIN   Mount Koya's mountain god in Shinto mythology. Koya-no-Myoin hunts with two hounds at his side.

KOYA-SHONIN   A Buddhist saint to whom many miracles are attributed. The most famous miracle occurred in 963, when *Koya* is credited with having ended an epidemic by building the Rokuharamitsu-Ji, a TEMPLE in KYOTO.

KOZUKO BOSATSU   A Japanese Buddhist BOSATSU, or BUDDHA-to-be, who helps others achieve ENLIGHTENMENT.

KUJAKU-MYŌ-Ō   One of the Buddhist MYŌ-Ō, or Kings of Light. Kujaku is unlike the other kings, who are fierce warriors who fight evil on behalf of specific Buddhas. Instead, he looks peaceful and sits on a peacock. It is said that praying to Kujaku during a drought will bring rain.

KŪKAI   (774–835) A Buddhist MONK who helped lay the ground for RYŌBU, or "Shinto with two faces," by identifying Buddhist deities with native Japanese Shinto divinities, or KAMI. He is also credited with establishing the Shingon, or "True Word," sect of Buddhism in Japan. After his death, he was honored with the title KŌBŌ DAISHI.

KUKUNOCHI-NO-KAMI   The SHINTO god of trees.

KUMASO In Japanese legend, the head of a group of bandits defeated by YAMATO-TAKERU.

KUMO Mythic SPIDERS in Japanese legend and folktales that are larger than men. Their eyes are the size of plates, their teeth like long and very sharp knives. Spiders play the role of demon in many stories. They are often found in old castles, and they sometimes imprison men with their sticky webs.

KUNG FU-TZU See CONFUCIUS.

KUNI-TOKO-TACHI One of the creators of earth in early Japanese myth. He lives on or in FUJI-SAN.

According to the SHINTO CREATION MYTH, Kuni-Toko-tachi reigned before the emergence of IZANAGI AND IZANAMI, during a brief, perfect period before the earth descended into chaos. He traveled to eastern lands to plant the seeds of trees. His descendants there ruled that land and venerated the early gods. When Izanagi and Izanami wed, they took vows mystically supplied by Kuni-Toko-tachi and were guided by his spirit in choosing a castle and restoring the ancient order of the earth.

KURA-OKAMI The SHINTO god of rain and snow.

KUSA-NADA-HIME The rice paddy princess. Kusa-nada-hime is the wife of the god SUSANO-WO.

KUSANAGI (KUSANAGI-NO-TSURUGI) Kusanagi, or "cutter of grass," is a descriptive name applied to a powerful, magical sword. The Kusanagi belongs to the imperial family and is said to have been a gift from the SHINTO god SUSANO-WO.

In SHINTO myth and legend, Kusanagi has enormous power; the warrior who wields it can single-handedly defeat an entire army. According to legend, YAMATO-TAKERU was given the sword by his father, the emperor, when he was sent to fight in the eastern parts of Japan. Yamato was tricked by the enemy and nearly killed by fire in a field. After he escaped, he used the sword to slay his enemies.

Another famous tale tells of the loss and recovery of the sword. Japanese forces were said to have lost a sea battle because Emperor Antoku Tennō, a baby at the time, was too young to hold the weapon. Rather than accept the shame of defeat, his grandmother Nu-no-ama took the boy and jumped with him into the water.

Many years later, Emperor Go Shirakawa called for the sword when his enemies threatened to attack. But the sword, which had supposedly been placed in a temple, could not be found. The emperor dreamed that an old woman came to him and said the sword was being held by the King of the Sea. In due time, the emperor sent divers to the area where Antoku Tennō had been drowned. The divers, a mother and a daughter named Omiatsu and Wakamatsu, dove into the water. At the bottom they found a dark cave. Entering it, they discovered a jeweled passage and a secret world.

Soon they came to a fabulous city. It was surrounded with gold walls and magnificent towers. The sea god's palace lay inside, but mother and daughter were stopped at the gates to the city. There, a holy man appeared and said they could not enter without BUDDHA's help.

The next day, assisted by special charms, they returned and reached the palace. Outside, two women made them look through a window beneath a pine tree. The pearl blinds on the window were slowly opened, and they saw the sword in the mouth of a massive snake. A little boy lay asleep in the snake's coils.

The snake spoke to them. It claimed that the sword did not belong to the emperor but had been stolen by a dragon-prince, who later lost it to a Japanese hero (presumably Susano-Wo). The Japanese hero gave it to the emperor. Years later, a sea dragon had taken the shape of a woman and married an emperor. She was the grandmother who jumped into the sea with Antoku Tennō.

The divers returned and told the emperor the entire story. A magician promised that a spell could help him retrieve the sword. The spell worked, and the emperor was able to use the sword to defeat his enemies. The sword was then placed in the temple of Atsuta for safekeeping.

Later, a Korean priest stole the powerful sword and tried to escape back to KOREA with it. But the sea god was angry and roiled the waves. Finally, the priest threw the sword overboard and the storm subsided.

The sea god retrieved the sword and placed it back in the temple, where it stayed for another hundred years. Then it was finally returned to the sea god's palace under the waves.

KWAIDON   Japanese ghost stories. These can be from any period.

KWANNON   Another name for KANNON.

KYOTO   Emperor KAMMU made Kyoto—at the time called Heian-kyo—the capital of Japan in 794, replacing the former capital of Nara. Kyoto remained the official capital for more than 1,000 years. It remains an important cultural and religious center.

As the seat of the imperial family, Kyoto was the spiritual and artistic center of the country as well as the center of government. Among its many distinctive features is the grid pattern of streets at its center, a relatively rare layout in ancient Japanese cities. Like Nara, it was modeled on Ch'angan, at the time the capital of China. (See CHINESE INFLUENCE.)

There are more than 2,000 SHRINES in the city. They are visited by millions of tourists every year. Among the most famous are Higashi Hongan-ji, which is said to have the largest wooden roof in the world, and Kiyomizu-dera, which commands an astounding view of the countryside.

Besides its many TEMPLES, artworks, and great natural beauty, Kyoto is known for its annual Gion-matsuri, a festival held every July in commemoration of a ceremony performed in A.D. 869 to end an epidemic. The high point of the celebration is the Yamaboko Juko celebration, July 17. The celebration dates from the early 17th century and features a large parade with colorful floats. Though it appears to have legendary and even mythic connections, historians point out that the festival actually began as a political commemoration by businessmen celebrating policies of open trade before the Tokugawa military government (1603–1867) tried to isolate Japan in 1612.

The capital was moved to EDO in 1868. Edo, which sits farther north on the coast of Japan, was renamed TOKYO, or "Eastern Capital." Kyoto remained an important ceremonial, religious, and even mythic city. During World War II, the United States refrained from bombing Kyoto because of its importance as a cultural and religious site, even though factories outside the center city made items for the war. Stray and erroneous bombings destroyed fewer than 100 buildings there, with the loss of approximately 80 lives. This was in great contrast to destruction elsewhere in Japan.

L

LAO TZU A Chinese philosopher who is believed to have lived in the beginning of the sixth century. Lao Tzu is called the father of TAOISM or Daoism), an important Chinese philosophy. However, some historians and scholars do not believe that Lao Tzu was an actual person.

LITTLE ONE INCH Another name for ISSUN-BOSHI, a popular hero of mythological stories.

LORD BAG OF RICE A name given to the hero HIDESATO, after he helped the DRAGON KING at LAKE BIWA.

LOTUS The lotus is a beautiful water flower in the same family as water lilies, which are more common in the United States. It is an important symbol in art, myth, and legend around the world. For Buddhists and many others in Asia, the lotus represents immortality and purity, as well as ENLIGHTENMENT. Scholars trace the symbolism to India, where the lotus is included in the descriptions of early myths.

Some Buddhists believe that the appearance of a new BUDDHA on earth is marked by the blossoming of a special lotus, and lotus flowers are included in many pieces of art and literature describing NIRVANA and paradise. Paintings of Buddha, for example, often show him sitting on a lotus flower.

LOTUS SUTRA A very important text for Japanese Buddhists. The important texts of BUDDHISM are called SUTRAS. These contain the teachings of Buddha or commentaries on his teachings. Different sects place emphasis on different sutras. MAHĀYĀNA, or "Greater Vessel," Buddhists pay special attention to the *Lotus Sutra*.

The sutra teaches that BUDDHA's essence is found in all things. It suggests that the way to become enlightened is through wondrous apprehension rather than logic. According to the teachings, *BOSATSU* (Buddhas-to-be) work to help others reach ENLIGHTENMENT. KANNON, the Buddhist god (or goddess) of mercy, is discussed at length in the sutra, and the deity's powers of compassion are lauded.

The *Lotus Sutra* is credited with great power itself. Several Buddhist legends say it can save people on its own, and at times it seems itself a deity. For example, one tale in the *KONJAKU MONOGATARI* tells of a man whose life was saved simply because he recited the first syllable of the sutra.

LUCKY SEVEN Another name for the SHICHI FUKUJIN.

M

MAGATAMA ("curved jewels") In SHINTO myth, a necklace made of jewels that was one of the three gifts given by AMATERASU to her grandson, the first emperor of Japan.

The necklace's full name is YASAKANI NO MAGATAMA. It is also known as shinshi and "bead strand."

The word is also used for sacred stones used in ceremonies and for other purposes in Shinto rites.

MAHĀYĀNA BUDDHISM Mahāyāna, or "Greater Vehicle" or "Greater Vessel," BUDDHISM refers to a group of Buddhist sects that have similar beliefs. Among the most important from a mythological point of view is the belief that it is possible for people to achieve ENLIGHTENMENT through the works of others. This makes possible a PANTHEON of Japanese BUDDHIST DIVINITIES.

According to Mahāyāna Buddhism, BUDDHA is one manifestation of a force that lives beyond ordinary human knowledge. It distances itself from the older, more conservative sects that it calls Hīnayāna, or "Lesser Vehicle" or "Lesser Vessel," Buddhism. This branch, which calls itself THERĀVADA, "the way of the elders," holds that enlightenment can be achieved only by the means outlined in the conservative texts.

According to Mahāyāna teachings, there is an eternal Buddha without beginning or end. Different manifestations of this force live as people, and there is always one manifestation present in the world. The founder of Buddhism, SHĀKA, or Siddhartha Gautama (as he was known before reaching ENLIGHTENMENT), was one of these Buddhas.

Those who reach NIRVANA and become enlightened can choose to stay on earth and help other people. They are called BODHISATTVAS, or future Buddhas; in Japanese, the term is BOSATSU. According to Mahāyāna beliefs, this selfless action would be more worthy than simply reaching Nirvana. In Japan, many of the stories of bodhisattvas were adapted from earlier stories, legends, and myths originating elsewhere, especially India and China. (See INDIAN INFLUENCE and CHINESE INFLUENCE.)

The universe described by Mahāyāna Buddhism consists of several plains. The highest contains no material form at all; very ancient Buddhas live here. One level down, form is dissolving; somewhat less old but still ancient Buddhas live here, awaiting passage to the higher realm.

Below these is the world of forms or matter. Here there are six more levels or destinies. (We might think of these more as different dimensions than separate worlds.) The highest contains many HEAVENS. This is where the different groups of gods and *bosatsu* live, each in its own heaven.

The second level is inhabited by humans—earth, as we know it. The third is the realm of ASURAS, titans from Hindu mythology who fight men and gods; in Japanese Buddhism they are seen as demons who fight TAISHAKU (the Japanese version of an ancient Indian god Indra). The fourth level is the realm of animals.

The fifth is the level of GAKI, or "hungry ghosts"—souls that must repent evil deeds or other KARMA. The final level is hell, inhabited by evil beings.

Several sects of Buddhism are included in the Mahāyāna branch of Buddhism. Among them are SHINGON, ZEN, and TENDAI, all of which are important in Japan. In general, Mahāyāna sects are accepting of supernatural phenomena that often accompany myths and legends.

MAITREYA See MIROKU BOSATSU.

MALLET In some legends, a mallet or hammer is considered a good luck omen and can grant wishes when struck on the ground. See the story of ISSUN-BOSHI ("Little One Inch") for an example.

MANEKI NEKO A good luck charm used by storekeepers to bring customers to their shops. The "beckoning cat" sits with one hand out, as if gesturing to someone to come in.

MAN WHO MADE TREES BLOOM, THE

The title in English of a popular Japanese folktale. There are many different versions, but in the basic tale, a humble woodsman finds a small starving dog. He and his wife rescue the dog and nurse it back to health. The dog then finds buried treasure in his yard. A jealous neighbor tricks the couple into lending him the animal. When it does not find treasure for him, he hits the small dog so hard that it dies.

Buddhist teachers often used stories to illustrate the religion's important values. "The Man Who Made the Trees Bloom" shows how kindness can be rewarded— and how jealousy often leads to trouble. *(From Yei Theodora Ozaki,* Japanese Fairy Tales, *1903)*

Heartbroken, the old couple bury the dog. A tree grows in its place. From its wood the man makes a bowl to grind rice cakes for the dog's grave. The bowl magically changes the rice into more gold.

Once again the jealous neighbor manages to trick the old couple into giving him the bowl. Of course, no gold appears when he uses it—just old junk. Infuriated, he destroys the bowl.

Heartbroken once more, the old man takes the ashes. These turn out to help things grow quickly, instantly making flowers bloom. A passing lord sees the miracle and rewards the old man and his wife with more gold.

Once again the jealous neighbor strikes. He sprinkles the ashes before the lord, trying to impress him. But this time, the ashes form a dust cloud and nearly choke the lord to death. The jealous neighbor is severely punished.

Besides being humorous, the tale illustrates Buddhist values, such as kindness and simplicity.

MANYOSHU (*Collection of Ten Thousand [or Myriad] Leaves*) An eighth-century collection of Japanese poetry. Standard versions are made up of 20 books of 4,520 poems. Scholars have used the collection to gather information about early Japanese myths as well as poetic traditions.

MARA According to Buddhist myth, Mara is the demon of all demons. At the moment that Prince Siddhartha Gautama was about to reach ENLIGHTENMENT, Mara tried to banish him from his place beneath the tree of enlightenment. The devil and his troops were bested in a titanic battle. This myth of BUDDHISM's early origins predates the religion's arrival in Japan.

MARISHI-TEN (MARISHA-TEN) In Buddhist mythology, Marishi is the queen of heaven and the dawn. In Japan, she is regarded as the goddess of war and victory. During the Japanese middle ages, warriors believed that she could make them invisible to the enemy.

In art, Marishi is seen riding on or with a wild boar. She can have as many as eight arms and three heads, one of which is a sow's. In some tellings, Marisha-Ten is a male god, though dressed in Chinese female clothing. He is invisible or can make himself invisible.

Outside Japan, the god's name is usually given as Marichi or, in Sanskrit, Uşas, meaning "ray of light."

MASAKA-YAMA-TSU-MI The SHINTO MOUNTAIN god who presides over very steep slopes.

MATCHA The powdered form of green TEA used in the TEA CEREMONY.

MATSUHIME Matsuhime is the heroine of a Japanese folktale concerning forbidden love between different classes in society.

Matsuhime was the daughter of an important member of the imperial guard, but not a member of royalty. Even so, a prince fell in love with her. They married against his parents' wishes, and for a brief time they were happy. But one day while the prince was away, his parents had the girl lured from their house and killed.

The prince searched for her for days without finding a trace. Then one night he saw her ghost in the grass. He followed the ghost to a small cottage, where she told him what had happened. He fell asleep; when he woke up, the hut was gone. All that remained was her skeleton on the ground. The prince renounced wealth and power and became a Buddhist MONK.

MATSURI A festival celebrating a SHINTO SHRINE. Most Shinto shrines in Japan host an annual or biannual *matsuri*. This special event features a procession through the local streets and celebrates the shrine's KAMI, or resident deity. During the parade, a portable shrine dedicated to the local *kami* is paraded. This spreads the *kami*'s goodwill and power to the entire area.

MATSUYAMA The heroine of a popular Japanese folktale. After Matsuyama lost her mother, she looked into a mirror and saw her mother's face. The girl's devotion to her mother is cited as an example for others to follow.

MAWAYA-NO-KAMI Male and female deities of the toilet and the related bodily functions in

SHINTO myth. The Mawaya-no-kami were born when the wastes of Izanami touched the earth. (See IZANAGI AND IZANAMI.) Mawaya-no-kami have power over ailments involving the eyes, teeth, and women's reproduction.

MEIJI, EMPEROR (MITSUHITO) (1868–1912) The Meiji emperor, the 122nd reigning emperor, led Japan at a critical time in its history, helping the country modernize and become an important power. *Meiji* (Enlightened Peace) is the name given to the period of Mitsuhito's reign. He also presided over a revival in SHINTO, which regained some of its former importance. His spirit is venerated at Meiji-jingu, the largest shrine in TOKYO. At the time of his reign, EMPERORS were considered KAMI, or deities.

MIKADO A term once used in the West to refer to the Japanese emperor. The word is no longer commonly used.

MIKO Shrine virgins; young women who serve as attendants at SHINTO SHRINES. Sometimes called altar girls, they perform ritual dances and other duties at larger shrines. Worshipers seeking good luck charms usually purchase these at shrines tended by the altar girls, who wear long white tops over long red skirts. Serving as a *miko* brings great honor to one's family.

The same word is used to refer to a female SHAMAN. According to ancient Shinto beliefs, the *miko* are possessed by the KAMI, who can speak through them. Shamans played an important role in ancient Japan.

The word also refers to small statues that were buried with EMPERORS during the KOFUN PERIOD. Made of clay, these statues are of women who may be priests or able to contact the gods—that is, shamans.

MIKOSHI The portable SHRINES used during special festivals celebrating SHINTO deities. During these rituals, known as MATSURI, the representation of the local KAMI is paraded through the village or town associated with it. The deity renews its blessings and protection for the community during these parades, which date back to the early days of Shinto.

MINAMATO The Minamato clan fought with the TAIRA clan to rule Japan during its feudal period in the mid- to late 12th century. (See FEUDALISM IN JAPAN.) Tales of battles from those days remain popular today, just as tales about knights still entertain European audiences. The conflict between the two clans ended with the GEMPEI WAR (1180–85).

MINKAN BUKKYO A term sometimes used by scholars to describe "folk" beliefs related to BUDDHISM. Such beliefs might include superstitions, legends, and myths not recognized or included in the formal teaching of the religion.

MINKAN SHINKO A term sometimes used by scholars to describe "folk" beliefs related to SHINTO, but not considered part of the main Shinto religion.

MIN-YO Japanese folk songs, usually referring to songs associated with different types of work. Some are very old and celebrate figures from myths, legends, and folktales. The songs are often humorous and can include off-color puns. While the work songs are associated with different laborers, they may be sung by different people at certain occasions. For example, a popular wedding song is an *oiwake-bushi*, or "fork-in-the-road song," once sung by horse drivers.

Villages have traditional min-yo called *ko-uta*, which are sung at the local festivals. These usually include many local references. Others are sung at different festivals celebrated throughout the country. For example, a group of *min-yo* sung at BON, or the Festival of Lanterns, are known as *bon-odori-uta*, "songs of the Bon Festival."

MIRO (MIROKU, MIROKU BOSATSU) In Japanese Buddhist belief, Miro Bosatsu is the BOSATSU, or future BUDDHA, who lives in Tushita HEAVEN. He is the eighth Buddha, known as "the friendly Buddha" and called Maitreya in India and elsewhere. He is an important figure in MAHĀYĀNA BUDDHISM.

Miro waits to be born as a human who will then go on to become Buddha. According to Buddhist myth, he will come to earth 5,670,000 years after Buddha entered NIRVANA.

MIRROR According to the SHINTO CREATION MYTH, the sun goddess AMATERASU saw her reflection in a *kagami*, or mirror, after she had fled into a dark cave from her brother SUSANO-WO. Intrigued, she came out and the earth was restored to light. This mirror was later given to her grandson when he was sent to rule the earth.

The mirror, called the YATA NO KAGAMI, is still possessed by the imperial family. It is an important symbol of the emperor. A small mirror is still used as part of the ceremony at a cave commemorating Amaterasu's return.

MISOGI The term in Japanese for CLEANSING as part of a ritual PURIFICATION.

MISOGI-KYO The belief that PURIFICATION ceremonies are needed to rid a person of impurities. A Buddhist wishing to find inner peace or live a balanced life must purify himself of emotions such as anger and lust. The purification rituals must be repeated periodically until the person achieves ENLIGHTENMENT.

Purification is also a regular part of SHINTO ceremonies. It is usually done as one enters a SHRINE.

MIYAZU-HIME According to SHINTO mythology, Miyazu-Hime is the wife of the god SUSANO-WO. There is a famous SHRINE dedicated to her in Atsuta. She is considered the goddess of royalty.

MIZUHAME-NO-MIKOTO A water deity. Mizuhame-no-Mikoto is Izanami's youngest child. (See IZANAGI AND IZANAMI.)

MOCHI Mochi cakes are made from RICE flour according to an ancient recipe. They play an important role in some Japanese traditions and are considered good luck to give and receive. Legend states that if one looks at the full moon carefully, he or she will see a RABBIT working diligently to make the cakes. *Mochi* means "full moon."

MOMOTARO The folk story of Momotaro, or the Peach Boy, has been told countless times, both in Japan and the West, and may be among the most

The story of Momotaro—"the Peach Boy"—has been translated into many different languages and told around the world. This illustration is from an English version of the tale. *(From Yei Theodora Ozaki, Japanese Fairy Tales, 1903)*

from his mother and went to liberate them. Along the way he met a dog, a pheasant, and a monkey. In exchange for the delicious dumplings, they agreed to go with him.

On the island, Momotaro found that the *oni* had captured many girls. He and his companions stormed the demons' castle. They killed the *oni* and freed the girls. They also found a great deal of treasure that the devils had stolen. All were returned to the local village.

MONJU-BOSATSU   In Japanese Buddhist myth, the BOSATSU, or future Buddha, of wisdom and knowledge.

A handsome young man, Monju is wise and kind. Monju-Bosatsu is the Japanese form of the Sanskrit Manjuśri. His name refers to his handsome features. In art, he is often shown on a lion holding a book and a sword.

MONK   A man bound by vows to a life of religious devotion. Buddhist monks renounce worldly goods. They are supposed to have very few possessions—a bowl, three robes, a belt, a razor, and a needle. Depending on the sect and tradition, a monk might wander from place to place living on the charity of others, or he might live in a monastery among fellow monks. This was especially true in ancient Japan, where monks and monasteries were important permanent features of the community and, in some cases, wielded great power.

While vows and practices differ from sect to sect and even monastery to monastery, in general by renouncing worldly desires a monk (or a nun, the female equivalent) also renounces physical love. Chastity is an important requirement for nearly all monks. But sex remains a great temptation, especially for those who are new to the holy life. It often plays a part in legends and stories, demonstrating how difficult it can be to stay on the path toward enlightenment.

Monks are sometimes featured as characters in Japanese legends, especially those with Buddhist themes or origins. While generally they are shown to be devout and to help people, some tales make fun of novice monks or show others giving in to temptation.

popular tales in the world. There are variations with every teller, but the following is the basic story.

One day an old couple found a peach floating in a stream. When they cut open the fruit, they discovered a small boy. They called him Momotaro, "the eldest son of a peach." Since they had been unable to have their own child, they raised him to be a great man and hero.

At the age of 15, Momotaro set out to find adventure. Hearing that ONI, or devils, were harming people on a nearby island, he took three dumplings

MONKEY   Monkeys appear in a variety of myths, legends and tales, often as helpful figures. In the story of MOMOTARO, for example, the hero is helped by a monkey.

MOON   In Japanese myth and legend, the Moon has several different identities. In the SHINTO creation myth, a male god identified with the Moon, TSUKIYOMI, slays INARI, the goddess of RICE and fertility, which leads to the growth of many different vegetables and grains. (Some sources list the moon god as female, giving Tsukiyomo as the name.)

Other Japanese legends tell of KAGUYAHINE, the child of a moon god who comes to earth. Japanese folktales sometimes tell of the Moon as being a land of RABBITS.

MOON-CHILD   Another name for KAGUYAHINE.

MOUNTAIN MAN   The mountain man is roughly the equivalent of America's Bigfoot in Japanese folklore. In stories and artwork, the mountain man is seen as a large, half-ape, half-human creature. He can be soothed by someone offering him a bowl of RICE.

According to the Shinto creation myth, the Moon and Sun never appear in the sky together because Amaterasu was disgusted by her brother Tsukiyomi's slaughter of Inari. (*Christopher Dresser,* Japan: Its Architecture, Art, and Art Manufactures, *1882)*

MOUNTAINS   Like other natural features in Japan, mountains are believed to have KAMI, or gods, associated with them. The mountain is seen as a manifestation or extension of the god itself, much as the body of a person is connected to his or her soul in many religious beliefs.

According to the SHINTO CREATION MYTH, the first mountain gods were created when Izanagi killed the fire god KAGUTSUCHI, whose birth had killed Izanami. (See IZANAGI AND IZANAMI.) Five gods sprang from the slain god. O-YAMA-TSU-MI was the first and is the leader of these mountain gods. NAKA-YAMA-TSU-MI is the *kami* of slopes, HA-YAMA-TSU-MI is the *kami* of the lower slopes, MASAKA-YAMA-TSU-MI presides over very steep slopes, and SHIGI-YAMA-TSU-MI stands at the foot of the mountain.

The story of the mountain gods' origin reminds us that many mountains in Japan are or were volcanoes, including the most famous mountain of all, Mount Fuji, or FUJI-SAN. In addition to Mount Fuji, other important mountains in Japan include Mount Aso, Mount Nantai, and Ontake-San.

Specific myths regarding mountains are ancient. Many involve hunters who prove their skills in the wildness of the mountain area. For example, in one ancient Japanese legend Mount Nikkō and Mount Akagi were fighting. Nikkō asked the hero BANZABURŌ to help her. The huntsman found a giant centipede as he trekked through the forest and shot out its eye. He then discovered the monster was actually Mount Akagi and received great honor and rewards.

MOUNTAIN WOMAN   According to some Japanese legends, an evil mountain woman dines on unfortunate travelers captured as they travel through her mountain domains. The size of a gorilla and just as strong, she can fly easily through the air. A mountain woman appears as a kind of bogey in stories.

MOUNT FUJI   The English name for FUJI-SAN.

MUJINTO   A group of islands off the southern coast of Japan that are now known as the Bonin or Ogasawara Islands. According to early Japanese legend, a tribe of giants once lived here.

MUSO KOKUSHI According to Japanese Buddhist legend, Muso Kokushi was a very devout MONK. One night while he was watching over a dead body, a JIKININKI or corpse-eater came to eat the body. Unafraid, the priest prayed so devoutly that not only did the *jikininki* fail to snatch the body, but the curse that held it was lifted. The *jikininki*'s soul was liberated to join the dead in heaven.

MUSUBI-NO-KAMI The god of love and marriage in SHINTO mythology. Young girls may meet Musubi-no-Kami as they walk near the sacred cherry tree, Kanzakura, where he lives. The handsome young god offers them a cherry branch and promises that they will soon wed their true love.

MUSUBI The concept of *musubi,* or "becoming," is central in Shinto and Japanese thought. It implies not just birth and creation but harmony and cooperation among different powers. The names of many *kami* incorporate the concept of *musubi.* For example, Takami-Musubi no kami and Kami-Musubi no kami are the gods of birth of heaven and earth. Along with Amenominakanushi no kami, deity of the center, these gods made possible the creation of heaven and earth.

MYŌ-Ō In Japanese Buddhist mythology, the Kings of Light. The Myō-ō help the BUDDHAS, usually by combating evil. They can also inspire humans and keep them from temptation.

FUDŌ is probably the best known Myō-ō in Japan and is often connected with the SHINGON sect of Buddhism. Other important ones are AIZEN, DAI-ITOKU, GOZANZE, GUNDARI, and KONGO-YASHA.

In art, the Myō-ō often appear with circles around their heads, or halos, a symbol of their light.

N

NAGA In Japanese mythology, *naga* are dragon-serpents that live at the bottom of the sea. Some scholars believe that the dragon palace that appears in myths and legends comes from Buddhist mythology and refers to a place where sacred scrolls are kept. On the other hand, there are many mythologies and legends concerning sea monsters and sea kingdoms throughout Asia not necessarily connected with BUDDHISM.

NAKATSU-HIME The Lady of the Middle World, who rules as SHINTO goddess of the eight islands below heaven.

NAKA-YAMA-TSU-MI The god or spirit of slopes in SHINTO mythology. He was one of five MOUNTAIN gods created when Izanagi killed KAGUT-SUCHI, the fire god whose birth had killed Izanami. (See IZANAGI AND IZANAMI.)

NAKISAWAME When Izanagi cried over the death of his wife, Nakisawame sprang from his tears. She is the "crying weeping female" and lives at the foot of Mount Kagu, according to the SHINTO CREATION MYTH.

See also IZANAGI AND IZANAMI.

NANAKUSA The Seven Grasses Festival, held each January 7. According to ancient beliefs, eating a special stew made of RICE and herbs on this day will ensure good health for the coming year.

NENBUTSU The incantation, or calling, of the BUDDHA. It was believed by many that saying AMIDA's name at death would lead to REBIRTH in the Pure Land. (See PURE LAND BUDDHISM.)

NE NO KUNI Another name for YOMI, the SHINTO underworld. The word may be translated as "land of the roots" in English.

NETHERWORLD See YOMI.

"NEW RELIGIONS" As Japan opened up to the West and modernized, it experienced a new round of pressures. The overthrow of the TOKUGAWA Shogunate, or military government, led to the MEIJI Restoration in 1868. This restored the EMPEROR to his ancient role as actual head of government, a role which for hundreds of years the imperial family had held in name only. SHINTO SHRINES once more became closely aligned with the government, which appointed the priests who oversaw them. The new constitution included a clause stating that the emperor had descended from the gods. Several ancient practices, especially those honoring ANCESTORS, were officially encouraged. A number of different new sects, such as TENRIKYO, sprang up. Most revived ancient traditions or used old Shinto methods for healing.

Defeat in World War II (1941–45) brought a new constitution to Japan, and the emperor was forced to renounce his divinity. The number of shrines began to decrease for various reasons as the religion once more responded to modern pressures. But the opportunities for new revivals remained. Several "new religions" sprang up that made use of ancient Shinto myths. For example, Munetada Kurozumi, the leader of the Kurozumi sect, began his new sect or cult following a mystic experience that involved union with Amaterasu. Other sect leaders spoke of mystic possessions by kami.

We are too close to these movements to know what sort of lasting myths they may or may not give rise to.

NEW YEAR FESTIVAL The annual celebration known as SHOGATSU-MATSURI, during which many Japanese visit SHINTO shrines.

NIHONGI (*NIHON SHOKI; Chronicles of Japan*) A history of Japan written in 720 that includes early SHINTO CREATION MYTHS. The *Nihongi* was written in Chinese characters, and scholars believe that it was heavily influenced by Chinese ideas and beliefs. (See CHINESE INFLUENCE.) Many of the stories are the same as or very similar to those in the *KOJIKI*, which was written in 712.

NIJUHACHIN BUSHU The 28 constellations known in ancient Japan. In Buddhist mythology, these groups of stars are considered servants of KANNON, the *BOSATSU* (future BUDDHA) of mercy.

NIKKŌ (NIKKŌ-BOSATSU) The BODHISATTVA of sunshine and good health in Buddhist myth. Nikkō and GAKKŌ, the bodhisattva of the Moon, often accompany YAKUSHI, the BUDDHA of healing.

NIKOBO According to Japanese legend, Nikobo was a powerful exorcist in Nikaido. By sending away evil spirits and demons, he could cure the sick and the possessed.

One day, the governor's wife became very sick. Fearing she would die, the governor sent for Nikobo. Nikobo worked his magic, exorcising the evil and making the governor's wife well again. When she rose, Nikobo expected payment. But the governor laughed and called for his guards to take Nikobo away and have him killed. The death sentence was carried out, but instead of dying, Nikobo became a ball of fire and rose to the top of a tree, where he stayed forever. Not long afterward, the governor himself died. The governor's physicians could not explain how he had been killed.

NINIGI-NO-MIKOTO (*NINIGI, NINIKINE*) The grandson of the sun goddess AMATERASU and the creator god TAKAMI-MUSUBI, Ninigi-no-mikoto is the ancestor of the Japanese emperor, according to tradition. He is known as the god of plenty and Prince-Ear-of-Rice, and is called the August Grandchild, the Great Land Divider, and the Great Land Master.

According to the SHINTO CREATION MYTHS, Ninigi was sent to rule the earth by his grandmother. Amaterasu gave Ninigi a MIRROR, a strand of jewels known as the MAGATAMA, and a sword called AMA-NO-MURAKAMO-NO-TSURUGI. All had special powers and mythic significance: The mirror is said to be YATA NO KAGAMI, the mirror that enticed Amaterasu to come out of her cave. The sword was the most powerful the world had ever seen. And gods had been born from other jewels on the strand.

Amaterasu then sent Ninigi and UZUME, the goddess of the dawn, to earth. They were stopped at AMA-NO-UKI-HASHI, the floating bridge, where Sarutahiko Ohakami ("the bridge guardian" or "the god of paths") blocked their way. Ninigi was scared, but Uzume was not. Uzume not only convinced him to let them pass, but the god fell in love with her and married her.

The myths say that Ninigi won many battles, conquering southern Japan and establishing his rule of order. Finally, on the Yamato plain, he established the imperial dynasty, with his wife KONOHANASAKUYA.

Ninigi was the father of HIKOHOHODEMI AND HONOSUSERI. His descendants became the emperors of Japan. The mirror, jewels, and sword given by Amaterasu to Ninigi-no-mikoto remain the imperial symbols in Japan.

NINYO A mermaid.

NIO In BUDDHISM, the two kings of compassion, Fukaotsu and Soko. The Nio are giant spirits that guard temple gates as well as monasteries. In art, they often look like ferocious beasts dressed in armor. Besides warding off evil spirits, they keep away thieves and guard small children.

NIRVANA Nirvana represents full ENLIGHTENMENT and the highest plain of existence for a soul in Buddhist belief. The word means "blow out" in its original Sanskrit form. Achieving Nirvana, the soul "blows out" all desire. Different sects of BUDDHISM have different ideas about what Nirvana is like.

NŌ (NOH) An important Japanese art form, Nō drama probably developed from the earlier *sarugaku*, a folk entertainment that served as a comic break from

Nō mask. *(Richard Huber,* Treasury of Mythological Creatures*)*

NOBUNAGA (ODA NOBUNAGA) (1534–1582) Nobunaga was a historical warlord and military leader whose conquests during the 16th century ended an era of warfare and reunited Japan. Nobunaga's troops made use of Western firearms and advanced tactics to defeat an array of enemies. Nobunaga was hostile to BUDDHIST sects, many of which had small armies at the time. He destroyed many Buddhist centers and persecuted their members. He was finally ambushed and murdered by a traitor. He was succeeded by HIDEYOSHI, one of the great leaders of Japan.

NOMINOSUKUNE The god of wrestlers in Japanese mythology.

NORITO Prayers used at SHINTO ceremonies. A collection of these prayers included in a book written in 927 called *Engishiki* is used by scholars studying ancient Shinto practices.

NURIKABE An invisible wall blocking a road. According to Japanese legends and folk beliefs, it lengthens journeys, making a trip of an hour last a whole day (or more). The wall has a magic ability to

SHINTO ceremonies, as well as *dengaku*, which had evolved from acrobatics and juggling to a form closer to opera. Scholars also have seen the influence of other forms of dance and singing on the art. The SHINTO priest Kanami (1333–84) is credited with inventing the art form for a performance he gave with his son Zeami (1363–1443) for Shogun Yoshimitsu (1358–1408).

In Nō theater, performers wear elaborately decorated costumes and masks that symbolize their emotions. Lines are chanted instead of spoken; they are both prose and poetry written in a very formal Japanese that dates to the medieval period of Japan. The actors dance in slow, highly ritualized steps on a small, square stage. A pine tree is painted on the back wall of the stage.

Many Nō plays use literature and themes from earlier periods and deal with myths and Buddhist themes.

One sign of wrestling's importance in ancient Japan was the fact that it had its own Shinto god, Nominosukune. Sumo wrestling combines athletic prowess with spiritual strength, so that the competitors are artists. This photo dates from the early 1900s, when wrestling was a community event in rural Japan. *(Library of Congress, Prints & Photographs Division [LC-USZ62- 097650])*

move. Pilgrims or travelers encountering a *nurikabe* usually have no way of knowing it until they discover they have taken much longer than expected.

NYO-I-RIN KANNON   The six-armed manifestation of KANNON. Kannon is considered both male and female, though statues of Nyo-i-rin usually show male characteristics.

NYORAI   "BUDDHA." The word is used as part of phrases describing different Buddha manifestations in the MAHĀYĀNA tradition. For example, Dainichi-Nyorai is the Great Sun Buddha.

O-ANA-MOCHI (OANOMOCHI) O-Ana-Mochi is the resident deity of the crater of FUJI-SAN, or Mount Fuji, the most famous MOUNTAIN in Japan and a volcano. (It last erupted in 1707.) At 12,389 feet, Mount Fuji is the highest mountain on Honshu, the central island of Japan.

OBON See BON.

ODA NOBUNAGA. See NOBUNAGA.

OFUDA A token that honors Japanese KAMI or Buddhist gods. A sheet of paper is folded in a special way around a stick of wood. The god's name is then written or printed on the paper. It is common for a visitor to a SHRINE to obtain one as a token of his or her devotion.

OHONAMOCHI SHINTO god of the earth.

OHO-YAMA The father of Iha-Naga and KO-NO-HANA. Oho-Yama is a mountain god in SHINTO mythology.

ŌJIN (200?–?310) Born to Empress JINGŌ and Emperor Chūai, Ōjin ruled as the 15th reigning emperor—or *tennō*—of Japan. Among his many accomplishments, he is credited by some with introducing writing to Japan. It is said that he invited Korean and Chinese scholars to his court to help educate his son, Nintoku, and that this brought writing to Japan. Among the tales associated with Ōjin are some that claim he would sneak from the palace to mingle with commoners and discover what was really going on in their country. Historical records show that he was regarded as an intelligent leader and great thinker.

After Ōjin's death, a shrine was built to him. Hundreds of years later, a priest had a vision about Ōjin. In the dream, he saw that Ōjin was really HACHIMAN, the Japanese god of war. From that point, archers and soldiers wore small charms shaped like swords to honor him. A large number of SHINTO shrines are dedicated to Hachiman.

According to legend, Ojin Tennō was in his mother's womb as she conquered the three kingdoms of Korea. He waited to be born until after she had completed the conquest and returned home—proof, she said, that he was truly a god.

Ojin was born with a red birthmark on his elbow. It resembled the shield archers wear on their arms to protect them from the spring of the string of the bow as they fire. It proved to be an accurate omen of his great skill in battle.

OKIKU According to popular legend, Okiku was a servant girl who worked for a strict master. After she broke a set of valuable plates, the master had her tied up and thrown into a well. Her spirit returned as an *okiku* bug, a worm whose body looks as if it is tied with silk threads.

Scholars have traced elements of this tale to a plague of these worms—which thrive in old wells—in the late 18th century.

OKUNINUSHI (O-KUNI-NUSHI) The SHINTO god of magic and medicine. Okuninushi symbolizes nature's rebirth; he died twice and came back to life.

Okuninushi's powers are demonstrated in the story of how he found his bride. His brothers met a RABBIT who had been flayed and was in great distress. The young men—there were 80 of them—were in a hurry to meet the princess Yakami, whom they all hoped to marry. Rather than helping the poor injured creature, Okuninushi's brothers told the rabbit to bathe in the ocean, then allow the wind to dry it. This literally rubbed salt into the rabbit's wounds and made it worse than ever.

Okuninushi then happened by. He took pity on the rabbit. He told it to soak its wounds in fresh water. Then, he said, it must rub its body in the pollen of kama grass. The cure worked. The hare was really a god, and he told Okuninushi that he, not any of his brothers, would marry the princess.

Jealous of the prophecy, Okuninushi's brothers set out to kill him. First, they heated a rock and rolled it down a hill. Okuninushi thought he was being attacked by a boar or wild pig. He grabbed the white-hot rock to wrestle it and was killed by the tremendous heat. But his mother, Kami-Musubi, brought him back to life. A short time later, Okuninushi was crushed by his brothers.

After he was reborn once again, Kami-Musubi told Okuninushi that he should hide in YOUL, the underworld. While he was there, Okuninushi met

Okuninushi was both emperor and god, playing an important role in Shinto myth. In one of the best-loved tales about him, he helps a hare who had been treated poorly, and his kindness is soon rewarded. *(From Yei Theodora Ozaki,* Japanese Fairy Tales, *1903)*

SUSANO-WO and his daughter Suseri-Hime. Susano-Wo was the storm god and had a very bad temper. He revealed just how bad his temper could be when he learned that Okuninushi was in love with Suseri-Hime: He made Okuninushi sleep in a roomful of snakes.

Suseri-Hime had given Okuninushi a magic scarf, and the snakes could not harm him. Next, Susano-Wo had him sleep in a roomful of poisonous CENTIPEDES and wasps. Once again Okuninushi emerged unharmed. Susano-Wo sent him into a field, then set fire to it. A mouse showed Okuninushi the way to a hole where he could wait out the flames.

Almost in spite of himself, Susano-Wo started to like the young man. But Okuninushi did not trust him. While Susano-Wo slept, Okuninushi tied the god's hair to the boards that supported his house. Then he took the god's sword, bow, and harp (koto). He took Suseri-Hime and ran back to the earth.

Susano-Wo woke when he heard the harp. As he leapt upward, his tied hair pulled down the house. Despite his rage, he realized that Okuninushi was a brave young man, and he had to admire him. He yelled after him, telling him to use his sword to fight his brothers and rule the world. Susano-Wo then gave his daughter to Okuninushi in marriage, finally accepting him as his son-in-law.

Okuninushi ruled the earth from a palace at Mount Uka. In later years, he was visited by two gods sent by AMATERASU. These gods said that her grandson would take his place as ruler. Okuninushi agreed, but only if he would be given a SHRINE at IZUMO. Amaterasu agreed. His two sons also agreed, although his younger son soon tried to rebel. Eventually, Amaterasu's grandson NINIGI-NO-MIKOTO ruled the entire earth.

Okuninushi is also known as Daikoku-sama, and is sometimes confused with DAIKOKUTEN, a Buddhist god and one of the SHICHI FUKUJIN.

ŌMA One of two brothers in a Japanese mountain legend that illustrates the importance of compassion. (See KOMA.)

OMAMORI A token or amulet that can protect the person who holds it. An *omamori* extends the blessing and protection of a KAMI or Buddhist deity. An *omamori* might be considered a combination religious medal and good luck charm. Today, *omamori* can be obtained from Shinto and Buddhist TEMPLES.

OMITSUNO According to ancient SHINTO mythology, the god Omitsuno rules the land on Japan's west coast where the gods hold their annual assembly. (See ASSEMBLY OF THE GODS.) Omitsuno originally expanded his small kingdom by lassoing islands from the bottom of the sea and pulling them up. He is a grandson of SUSANO-WO.

ONAMUJI In SHINTO mythology, an earth god, the son of SUSANO-WO.

ONI Big-mouthed, three-eyed monsters or devils who haunt the wicked, stealing their souls when they die. About the size of humans, *oni* have horns and sharp nails and can fly. Some say they have the heads of horses or oxen. It is also said that a woman overcome with grief or jealousy may be turned into an *oni*. *Oni* sometimes appear in art and legends as bogeymen scaring children.

Nichiren, a Buddhist sage, believed that *oni* caused war, earthquakes, and eclipses.

The demons can be expelled by a special ceremony, called the *oni-yarabai*, which is held every year.

ONMYŌ (ONMYŌ-DŌ) Also known as YIN-YANG and yin-yang magic, this is a collection of ancient fortune-telling and astrology arts used by Taoist astrologers. (See TAOISM.) Today we might think of those who used them as magicians as well as astrologers. The magicians are called Onmyō-Ji and Shōmon-ji. Their arts, which included healing and predicting the future, were very important in ancient Japan.

ONMYŌ-JI Someone who uses ONMYŌ to tell the future.

ONOKORO The first island or landmass created by IZANAGI AND IZANAMI in the SHINTO CREATION MYTH. The primordial gods created it by dipping a magic, jeweled spear into the shapeless waters of earth.

ORAL TRADITION The handing down of myth or legend through stories told but not written

Onmyō fortune-tellers were very popular in ancient Japan. In this illustration special sticks *(zeichu)* are used to see the future. The drawing dates from the 19th century and is of a rural scene in Japan. *(Stewart Culin, Korean Games, 1895)*

down. Scholars note that while oral traditions are often accurate, they are subject to much change as the story is passed on. Details, therefore, can be unreliable.

Early Japanese myth was passed down by oral tradition until the early eighth century, when the KOJIKI was written. (Another such collection of tales, the NIHONGI, was written less than a decade later.) Until then, *katari-be* (bards) worked in a tradition also found in many other cultures, entertaining at banquets and on other occasions. Writing was not introduced into Japan until the fifth century.

The texts make it clear that the myths they tell existed for some time before they were written. They mention that there are different versions of what happened, which indicates that there were several ancient traditions that came together to make the overall myth. Writing down the myth helped the YAMATO clan shape the versions that best supported their authority. After the accounts of the gods are accounts of the gods' children—the emperors and those who helped them subdue the earth and unite Japan.

OSORE-ZAN An important mountain in northern Japan whose name means "fear mountain." According to ancient folk belief, the area marks the boundary between the living and dead worlds. Dead children are said to pile stones in the wilderness there.

Souls that stay too long on the shore are carried off to hell by demons. The *BOSATSU JIZŌ*, however, rescues as many as he can find.

OTOGI ZOSHI Japanese folktales. As a general rule, these concern members of the lower classes. They often have supernatural themes. Many are very humorous; some were used to illustrate religious and ethical points. *Otogi zoshi* have been very popular from ancient times and remain so to this day.

OTOHIME Another name for TOYOTAMA.

OTOKU-SAN A good luck doll, which, according to folk beliefs, may have magic powers. See TOKUTARO-SAN.

O-USU-NO-IKOTO The name of the hero YAMATO-TAKERU before he proved himself in battle.

O-YAMA-TSU-MI A SHINTO mountain god. O-Yama-Tsu-Mi was born when Izanagi cut the fire god KAGUTSUCHI into pieces following the death of his wife, Izanami. (See IZANAGI AND IZANAMI.)

OYA-SHIMA-GUNI When IZANAGI AND IZANAMI first made the earth, eight islands formed from the original ocean. These islands were called Oya-shima-guni, "the parent island country."

P

PEACH BOY   An English name for MOMOTARO.

PEACHES   Peaches are often a symbol of longevity in Japanese art and legends. In the tale of IZANAGI AND IZANAMI written in the *KOJIKI*, peaches are used by Izanagi to ward off demons. Some who study myths believe this is a sign of CHINESE INFLUENCE at the time the story was written. In Chinese myths and legends, peaches and peach trees often ward off evil spirits.

In the story of MOMOTARO, a boy is born in a peach and raised by an old couple. He becomes a great hero.

PEARL PRINCESS   The daughter of TOYOTAMA, the sea god, who married HIKOHOHODEMI in SHINTO myth. She is also known as the Abundant Pearl Princess.

POIYAUNPE   An AINU hero whose adventures are detailed in the *Kotan Utunnai*, a long song epic. According to the legend, as Poiyaunpe grew up in rural Japan, he heard the sounds of different gods. Sensing conflict and unsure of himself, he asked his stepmother about his identity. She told him that his real parents were killed during a fight with her people. The boy took his clothes and ran away. His stepmother followed and together they fought a number of monsters. Poiyaunpe met other allies along the way, including a female SHAMAN who eventually returned with him to his native people.

PRINCE SHŌTOKU   See SHŌTOKU.

PURE LAND BUDDHISM   A group of Buddhist sects that developed during the KAMAKURA PERIOD (1185–1333), a time marked by war and great suffering in Japan. According to their beliefs, a person who is dying can be taken to Jōdo, or "the Pure Land," by saying AMIDA's name at death; Amida is the BUDDHA of boundless light.

The sects believe that humans exist in an impure, unholy place where emotions rule. To escape the endless cycle of REBIRTH, humans must leave that place and enter a land where ENLIGHTENMENT is possible.

According to Pure Land Buddhists, this land is a paradise called Sukhāvatī in Sanskrit. They believe the soul can enter this place by meditation and chanting Amida's name. Arrival in the Pure Land is not quite the same thing as becoming enlightened, though it makes it possible.

The Pure Land sects were extremely popular from the end of 12th century onward and many still follow their beliefs. Jōdo-shū was the largest of the different schools.

PURIFICATION RITES   Just as we wash our hands before eating, according to Japanese tradition the soul, too, must be purified before undertaking certain activities, especially religious ones. CLEANSING RITUALS are often performed before entering TEMPLES or SHRINES. For example, when people enter a SHINTO shrine, they first purify their hands with pure water and then lightly rinses his mouth. This purifies the body so that it is ready to meet the *KAMI*.

In ancient Shinto beliefs, purification was necessary after a person did certain actions or came in contact with certain things. For example, coming in contact with the dead would make it necessary to purify oneself. Impurity could anger the gods, but it was not quite what westerners would consider a sin.

In Japanese BUDDHISM, PURIFICATION RITES could be used to rid a person of demons and of overwhelming desires. These desires may prevent him or her from reaching ENLIGHTENMENT.

Purification often is symbolized by the act of cleansing with water. But incense and other tokens can be used in the ritual.

Even when the act of purification involves physically cleaning the body, it is important to remember that this is also a symbol of spiritual cleansing. The soul or the divine part of the body is being made ready for a spiritual experience. Purification prepares the soul to be renewed and reenergized.

The Shinto myth of IZANAGI AND IZANAMI contains an important example of purification. Upon his return from the underworld, Izanagi must purify himself before he can continue creating lesser gods and the rest of the universe.

R

RABBIT Rabbits or hares appear in several Japanese folktales and legends, usually helping mankind. In a story included in the *KOJIKI*, a rabbit

Rabbits often help humans in Japanese folktales and myth. This woodcut illustrates the story of the Badger and the Rabbit. *(From Yei Theodora Ozaki,* Japanese Fairy Tales, *1903)*

tricks a group of crocodiles into helping him across to the mainland from Oki. The hare loses his fur in the process but is helped by OHKUNINUSHI, a young man who uses pollen to restore his white hair. The grateful rabbit then helps Ohkuninushi win the hand of a princess.

In another tale, a rabbit helps avenge the death of an old woman by tricking a wily BADGER; the badger had not only killed the woman but made soup from her and tricked her husband into eating it. The rabbit's punishments are very cruel: he burns the badger and then sticks red pepper on its wounds, all the time pretending to be a friend. Then he kills the evil badger. His actions are justified by the badger's evil deeds, which must be punished.

RAIDEN *Rai* means "thunder"; *den* means "lightning." Raiden is the SHINTO god of both. It is said that he saved Japan from invading Mongols in 1274 by sending lightning to destroy the attacking fleet. Raiden's skin is red. He has sharp claws but cannot harm anyone hiding beneath a mosquito net.

RAIJIN A thunder god. According to Buddhist myth, FUJIN and Raijin stood together against the gods, until BUDDHA himself ordered their capture. It took 33 gods to defeat them. At the end of the battle, Fujin and Raijin were converted to BUDDHISM.

RAIJU A "thunder beast"; an animal that is blamed for the damage lightning does when it strikes the earth. Different sources picture the *raiju* as a CAT, weasel, or BADGER.

Raiden's lightning bolts can cause terrible damage, but the Shinto god also helped ancient Japan stave off attack. *(Christopher Dresser,* Japan: Its Architecture, Art, and Art Manufactures, *1882)*

RAIKO (REIKO)

The name used in Japanese legends for YORISUNE, an 11th-century hero and member of the MINAMOTO clan, which vied for control of Japan. The tales credit him with killing many giants and evil monsters, though in real life he fought another clan for domination of Japan. The legends and tales dwell more on the fame of the real fighter than his history, in roughly the same way King Arthur is believed to be based on a real hero in Great Britain.

Raiko has a group of brave SAMURAI fighting for him. These warriors have adventures of their own. Among the best known in the West is WATANABE NO TSUNA, who fights an *ONI* (sometimes translated "ogre" or "demon") at the Gate of Rashōmon.

Following is a typical Raiko tale.

One day, Raiko followed a skull into an old building. There, three women appeared in succession—an old witch, a nun, and then a beauty. Overcome by the woman's beauty, Raiko stared at her—until he suddenly found himself covered by a web. Raiko drew his sword and tried to free himself, but the metal broke when he struck the beautiful woman. She disappeared, leaving him still trapped.

Watanabe arrived and managed to free him. The two warriors searched for the woman, but could only find an immense spider—with the tip of Raiko's sword in its belly. The two men cut open the dead spider. The skulls of its victims were in its stomach. So were baby spiders—more demons. Raiko and Watanabe went to work killing them quickly. Their victory freed the countryside from a reign of evil.

RAITARO

According to an ancient Japanese folktale Raitaro, or the Thunder Baby, brought prosperity and good luck to a peasant farmer named Bimbo. Bimbo discovered Raitaro one day after a rainfall broke a severe drought. Bimbo raised the boy as his own son and was never again threatened by drought. Raitaro had the power to order rain whenever it was needed. When he became a man, Raitaro was transformed into a white DRAGON and left his adopted home.

Raiko was based on a real hero—Yorisune—but many of his legends are fiction. Here he confronts a serpent in one of his fictional adventures. *(From Yei Theodora Ozaki,* Japanese Fairy Tales, *1903)*

RAKAN BUDDHA's followers, the Rakan, are often used in BUDDHIST stories as examples of true believers. Traditionally, there are 16, including BINZURU, who was denied entrance to NIRVANA because of a sin during his youth. The true believers are contrasted with Chodatsu (or Devadatta), a man who renounced Buddha and committed so many sins that he was taken to hell while still alive.

RASHŌMON A famous gate in the city of Nara. (See WATANABE.)

REBIRTH AND REINCARNATION The idea that a soul returns to life in another body after the first body's DEATH. Rebirth is an important element of Buddhist belief. In each life, a soul can seek to advance through the different spheres of existence, until finally it reaches ENLIGHTENMENT, or NIRVANA. The cycle of life and death is known as samsara.

Exact beliefs about rebirth differ depending on sect, but, in general, a soul must do good deeds and follow its KARMA, or destiny, to move toward a higher sphere. Many Asian religions and myth systems include such beliefs. Many popular legends also refer to it, without being myths themselves. Here is one:

A young man and a woman who loved to garden married. For many years, they lived and gardened together. Theirs was a very happy marriage. But they did not have any children until they were well past middle age, when they had a son. They raised him to love gardening, and together they lived very happily. Then, the man and woman died. Their son worked in the garden as they had shown him. One day, he noticed that there were two butterflies in the garden. That night, he dreamed he saw his mother and father in the garden, inspecting the plants. In his dream, they turned into butterflies. The next morning, he saw the same butterflies fluttering between the plants. He knew the butterflies were the reincarnated souls of his parents.

RICE In ancient times rice was an extremely important food for the Japanese, and it is still a regular part of their diet. Its importance in Japan is emphasized in many myths and ancient religious ceremonies. Offerings of rice are usually made to ancestors and other KAMI.

SHINTO ceremonies to help its cultivation date back thousands of years. Even today, growing rice is considered one of the most important jobs a person can have. The emperor personally conducts a ritual each year that is said to encourage a successful rice crop.

INARI is the Shinto god of rice.

RŌNIN Samurai warriors who have lost their master. Such a soldier was looked down upon and was often homeless as well as unemployed. *Rōnin* appear in stories and legends from the medieval time, some based on historic fact, that celebrate BUSHIDŌ, or the warrior's way.

The most famous story concerning *rōnin* is popularly known as "The 47 *Rōnin*" and celebrates the revenge of the warriors on behalf of their master. One of the best-known accounts of the incident is a Japanese Kabuki drama called *Kanadehon Chushingura* (*The Treasury of Loyal Retainers: A Model for Emulation*). The names of the principals and the setting were altered in the play because of government restrictions, but the basic tale was based on historic fact.

In 1701, a dispute between Asano Takumi no kami Naganori (1667–1701) and Kira Kozukenosuke Yoshinaka (1641–1702) led to an attack by Asano on Kira in the palace of Shogun Tokugawa Tsunayoshi. Asano was arrested and sentenced to commit ritual suicide. His family's fief was also forfeited. Asano's samurai—now *rōnin*, as their leader had died—vowed revenge. They waited for months until the time was right. Then 47 *rōnin* who had followed Asano charged Kira's mansion in Edo, defeated Kira's men, and cut off his head with the knife Asano had used to kill himself. They then turned themselves in and were later sentenced to kill themselves by ritual suicide. They were buried together and soon became the subject of legend.

RYŌBU-SHINTO (RYOBU, RYŌBO-SHINTO, RYŌBU) The doctrine or idea of "SHINTO with two faces" or "Shinto with two halves." The doctrine allowed for the intermixing of Shinto and BUDDHIST beliefs. According to this theory, the Shinto gods are manifestations of Buddhist gods, and the world described in the Shinto myth is a version of the worlds described in Buddhist cosmology. There are also connections between Shinto and Buddhist rituals and other beliefs. In a way, Shinto was seen as Buddhism written in another, earlier language.

Credited to the Buddhist MONK Kōbō DAISHI, Ryōbu was a compromise that allowed Buddhism and Shintoism to exist together from the eighth century onward. Ryōbu placed Shinto SHRINES in Buddhist TEMPLES. Buddhist monks took over the ceremonies at most Shinto shrines.

Ryōbu-Shinto is also called Shingon Shinto, after the Buddhist SHINGON sect.

RYUGU   The palace of RYUJIN, the god of the sea, located at the bottom of the ocean according to SHINTO myth. The magnificent building is made of red and white coral. Each side of the palace is associated with different seasons and wonders. The Winter Hall on the north side, for example, is always covered with falling snow. The Hall of Spring on the east has cherry blossoms in bloom. Crickets chirp in the south-facing Summer Hall. In the Autumn Hall, at the palace's west face, maple leaves turn majestic red and yellow hues in the west. The palace is guarded by dragons.

RYUJIN   Ryujin is the god of the sea in ancient SHINTO myth. He lives at RYUGU, his palace, where he is waited on by half-human fish. Among his many powers is the ability to control the tides with special TIDE JEWELS. Ryujin's daughter TOYOTAMA married the divine hero HIKOHOHODEMI.

RYŪO   DRAGON KINGS in Japanese Buddhist myth, considered protectors of Buddha. Ryūō live

Urashima meets the daughter of the sea king in Ryugu, her father's palace. Urashima is sometimes called a Japanese Rip Van Winkle. *(From F. Hadland Davis, Myths & Legends of Japan, 1913)*

under the water or are somehow connected with it. As in other Japanese myths, these dragon or serpent kings can be helpful to humans or not.

S

SAE-NO-KAMI   In SHINTO myth, the gods who oversee the roads and highways.

ŚĀKAYAMUNI   See SHĀKA.

SAMBO-KOJIN   Sambo-kojin has three faces and two hands—very handy when you are the god of the kitchen. Sambo-kojin is a member of the SHINTO PANTHEON.

SAMEBITO   A fierce black monster with green eyes, Samebito was banished from the ocean by the sea king according to Japanese legend. In sorry shape, he tried to find shelter on a bridge. There he met Totaro and begged the hero to give him food. Totaro, who had expected to have to fight the monster, took pity on him instead. He brought Samebito home to his palace and put him in a lake.

Samebito grew strong again and was happy to have found a new home. But one day he discovered that his master lay sick in bed. Totaro had hoped to marry a beautiful princess named Tamana, but her father insisted he pay him 10,000 precious stones first—far too high a price even for Totaro.

Samebito wept bitterly at the news that his friend would die. His tears fell as emeralds and other jewels, which he gladly gave to Totaro, repaying his kindness. Totaro took them and ransomed Tamana for his bride.

SAMSARA   The idea that a soul returns to life in another body, or REINCARNATION.

SAMURAI   Samurai were Japanese warriors during Japan's feudal period (see FEUDALISM IN JAPAN). While not noblemen themselves, they were led by members of the aristocratic class and occupied a social position above commoners. The samurai were bound by personal loyalty to their leader. This tie was so great that it was considered honorable to commit suicide if one's leader died in battle.

A samurai was supposed to live according to a code of chivalry called Bushido, "The Warrior's Way." The perfect samurai was an intelligent, sensitive man who not only knew how to use a sword but appreciated fine art and poetry.

Samurai dressed in special armor made of scaled iron. A suit weighed about 25 pounds and was considerably more flexible than European armor of roughly the same period. Samurai fought with two swords: a long one and a shorter one ideally used for chopping off the head of a slain opponent. Their battle masks were shaped into ferocious faces. However, the warrior's helmet smelled sweet; prior to a battle, the samurai burned incense in it.

SANGANICHI   The Japanese new year. On this occasion, it is customary to clean house and then pray to the SHICHI FUJUKIN for luck in the coming year.

SANNŌ   The "King of the Mountain"; the guardian god for the TENDAI sect of BUDDHISM. The guardian gods protect the faithful from harm.

The Tendai sect was very influential in early Japan.

SANNŌ SHINTO   A Buddhist view of SHINTO beliefs that accepted the latter as another way of stating the basic beliefs of BUDDHISM. According to this view, AMATERASU was the creator of the universe and simply another way of thinking or talking about the never-ending BUDDHA that created the world. Members of the TENDAI Buddhist sect perfected the idea of Sannō Shinto and helped meld the two religions together. Sannō Shinto is also known as Tendai Shinto, and its effect was similar to "Shinto with Two Faces" or RYŌBU-SHINTO.

SANSHU NO JINGI   See THREE TREASURES.

SANZU NO KAWA   In Buddhist mythology, the river of three crossings that souls must cross after death; also called Watarigawa. The most difficult crossings must be taken by the worst sinners.

SARUDAHIKO   An earth god whose radiance is visible from great distances. Sarudahiko guided NINIGI-NO-MIKOTO on his journey to earth, according to SHINTO mythology.

Sarudahiko is seen as a model servant to the emperor. He also symbolizes masculinity. He has a red face, large round eyes, and a very long nose.

SARUTAHIKO OHKAMI   The guardian of AMA-NO-UKI-HASHI, or the floating bridge, the path from heaven to earth, in the time before AMATERASU sent NINIGI-NO-MIKOTO to rule the earth. The last of the earthly gods who remained opposed to Ninigi, Sarutahiko Ohkami refused to leave the bridge.

None of the heavenly gods was willing to challenge him—none of the male gods, at least. Finally, UZUME, the goddess of the dawn, rose and said she would confront him herself. She strode confidently to the bridge. When she reached it, she danced, showing off her grace and beauty to the large, powerful god. Impressed, Sarutahiko Ohkami listened as Uzume demanded that he give his loyalty to Ninigi. Sarutahiko did so and then asked if Ama-no-Uzume would marry him.

The goddess agreed, and the union was a happy one.

A SHINTO shrine honoring the tombs of these two gods was built at Tsubaki Dai Jinja in Mie Prefecture. Now more than 2,000 years old, the shrine remains to this day.

Sarutahiko Ohkami is seen in art as a massive giant with a long beard. Light shines from his body. He carries a jeweled spear. He is seen as a god of pathways and crossroads, including symbolic ones that are difficult to conquer.

SEIMEI   (911–1005)   Seimei was a Taoist doctor or magician. According to legend, he was able to use his skills to see if an illness would be fatal. In some cases, he was then able to save the lives of his patients by practicing his secret arts.

SENGEN-SAMA   According to SHINTO mythology, the goddess who guards the fountain of youth on FUJI-SAN; anyone who drinks its water has eternal life. Sengen-Sama lives at the top of the mountain and is also regarded as the blossom goddess.

A SHRINE to Sengen-Sama sits at the top of FUJI-SAN. Worshipers there greet the rising morning sun; Sengen-Sama is sometimes called Asama, which means "dawn of good luck." Her shrine remains an important place for pilgrims and tourists to visit.

Sengen-Sama is identified with KONO-HANASAKUYA, or "the Princess Who Makes the Tree Blossom Bloom," who married NINIGI-NO-MIKOTO. The two deities seem to have been separate at one time. Their linking is mentioned in HOTSUMA-TSUTAE, or *The Book of Heaven*, an ancient epic poem ostensibly written during the time of the legendary emperors.

SENJU KANNON   A manifestation of KANNON, an important *BOSATSU* in Japanese BUDDHISM. He is usually shown with 1,000 arms. The palm of each of his hands contains an eye, symbolizing that his compassion is everywhere and always ready.

SENNIN   Devout hermits who purify themselves by hard living in the mountains or wilderness. According to Japanese Buddhist belief and popular tradition, they can become *BOSATSU* (future BUDDHAS) through their great piety. Their spirits then live on and can perform many miracles.

There are a number of stories involving *sennin*. One famous *sennin* was Kume-no-Sennin, who lost his magic powers after staring at the feet of a woman washing clothes in a stream. His attention to earthly pleasures had cost him his divinity. But according to the tale, Kume-no-Sennin made the most of his predicament—he married the girl.

SENSU   The Japanese folding fan. According to legend, the *sensu* was invented in the seventh century after a craftsman saw how the wings of a bat worked.

A *sensu,* or folding fan.

In the Land of Perpetual Life, Sentaro discovered that everyone actually wished for DEATH. Things that were healthy in his homeland were poisonous here, and vice versa. After 300 years, he grew tired of this and decided to pray to leave. A paper crane appeared; it unfolded into the magic crane. But as he was heading back to Japan, Sentaro changed his mind. He could not stop the bird, however, and he fell in the ocean instead, where a large shark spied him and closed in for the kill.

At the moment, Sentaro woke up. He was still in the temple. It turned out that he had fallen asleep while praying. A messenger sent from the gods handed him a book of Buddhist scriptures, telling him the way of perpetual life was contained there. Grateful, Sentaro changed his lazy ways, studied the scriptures, and prospered.

Three to 25 ribs made of bamboo form the skeleton of the *sensu.* Bamboo paper is stretched across the ribs. Folded, it looks like a neat stack of thick paper or cardboard. Open, a *sensu* can be an impressive work of art.

The fan often appears in Japanese art, especially in drawings or paintings of court life, where women hold it near or over their faces. In real life, the fans are often pieces of art themselves. They often have scenes or symbols from legend and myth. A sun, for example, symbolizes Japan and the Shinto sun goddess AMATERASU and is a common motif.

SENTARO The hero of a Japanese folktale, Sentaro was a man who did not want to die but was otherwise lazy and vain. The tale has a Buddhist moral about the way to properly achieve everlasting life.

Hearing that hermits lived forever, Sentaro decided he would try to become one. He went to a TEMPLE and prayed for seven days. Finally, the temple god appeared. After pointing out that Sentaro liked life and material goods far too much to be a hermit, the god decided to grant his request in a different way. A crane appeared to carry Sentaro on his back to the Land of Perpetual Life.

Sentaro unfolded a paper crane and was transported from the world of eternal life. *(Collected by William Anderson in* Japanese Wood Engravings, *1908)*

SEPPUKU A form of ritual suicide performed to avoid dishonor. Real and legendary warriors during the feudal age (see FEUDALISM IN JAPAN) considered *seppuku* an honorable way to die.

SEVEN GODS Another name for the SHICHI FUKUJIN.

SHĀKA (SHĀKA-NYORAI, SHAKA) The Japanese name for the historical BUDDHA, Prince Siddartha, who founded BUDDHISM. He is considered a manifestation or a physical incarnation of the infinite Buddha in MĀHĀYANA BUDDHISM.

Every monastery contains a shrine to Shāka. A festival honoring Shāka called Hana-Matsuri, or the Flower Festival, is held April 8.

In Sanskrit, Shāka is known as Śākayamuni.

SHAMAN AND SHAMANISM Scholars use the word *shamanism* to describe a religion where a priest or shaman uses special powers to cure the sick and communicate with the spirit world.

In early Japan, shamans were very important members of the religious community. They held ceremonies and healed the sick. The shamans worked with specific clans and honored SHINTO gods. Most, though not all, were women. In all cases, they were believed to have special powers.

With the arrival of BUDDHISM, Buddhist MONKS also acted as shamans, casting out demons, telling the future, and performing other acts that we might consider magic.

Shamans often go into trances and repeat elaborate rituals as they communicate with the other world. They can rely on magic as well as religious traditions to do their job.

SHICHI FUJUKIN The seven popular Japanese gods of good luck or happiness. They were derived from a number of different sources.

Shichi Fujukin means "seven happiness beings." The gods are BENTEN, BISHAMON, DAIKOKU, EBISU, FUKUROKUJU, HOTEI, and JUROJIN. They were grouped together in the 17th century by a monk who wanted them to symbolize the best characteristics a person should have. These can be described as generosity, charity, openness, dignity, friendliness or popularity, age, and cheerfulness. The grouping may have been influenced by a similar grouping of Taoist (see TAOISM) figures often used by MONKS as teaching aids.

In Japan the Shichi Fujukin are honored every New Year (January 1–3).

SHICHI-GO-SAN Shichi-go-san, or "Seven-five-three" in English, is a kind of SHINTO national birthday festival for girls seven and three and boys five years old. Held each November 15, the festival is a way of thanking KAMI for protecting the children as they grow and asking for more good luck in the future. During the feudal period (see FEUDALISM IN JAPAN), the date marked the first time a young boy might dress in the special *hakama* (a divided skirt; a garment comparable to a cowboy's chaps) that SAMURAI wore (if he was entitled to do so by birth).

SHIGI-YAMA-TSU-MI One of the five SHINTO mountain gods. Shigi is the KAMI of the foot of the mountain.

SHIKO-ME In SHINTO mythology, female demons who inhabit YOMI, the underworld. The word means "ugly women."

SHINA-TSU-HIKO The god of the wind. Shina-Tsu-Hiko fills the space between the earth and HEAVEN. He also holds the earth in place with his wife Shine-to-Be. In the SHINTO CREATION MYTH, the gods were born when Izanagi (see IZANAGI AND IZANAMI) blew away the mist that covered the land. The pair are the principal Shinto WIND GODS.

SHINDA The AINU fertility god. Traditionally, believers thanked Shinda for providing food before each meal.

SHINDEN The inner sanctuary of a SHINTO SHRINE, where the KAMI may choose to dwell.

SHINE-TO-BE SHINE-TSU-HIKO's wife.

SHINGON A sect of BUDDHISM that refers to itself as "True Word" Buddhism. Shingon practices include elaborate rituals. It celebrates parts of existence that cannot be known intellectually and so is open to ideas about magic and the supernatural.

Symbols are an important part of art in this tradition, used to illustrate things that are beyond simple words or pictures. These may be temporary drawings on the ground, carvings, wall paintings, or scrolls.

Shingon Buddhism came to Japan in the year 806 when a priest named Kukai (774–835) returned from a trip to China with lessons learned there. (See CHINESE INFLUENCE.) Its popularity spread rapidly. Shingon's open acceptance of the supernatural may have helped Buddhism and Shinto fuse. It provided a way to accept Shinto legends and myths rather than attack them. (See RYŌBU-SHINTO.) Praised by the ruling powers, its popularity and influence spread rapidly.

SHINSHI   See YASAKANI NO MAGATAMA.

SHINTO   Shinto means "Way of the Gods." The Shinto religion dates from very early Japan, though experts disagree on its exact origin.

KAMI are the central focus of Shinto practices. While the word *kami* is generally translated as "gods" or "deities," the concept is actually very complex. All natural phenomena, such as mountains, streams, and volcanoes, have *kami*, or gods, associated with them. Each family also has ancestor gods, or *kami*. People who die become *kami*, joining the ancestral clan after a period of time if they are suitably honored.

Each community venerates its local gods at *jinja*, or SHRINES, dedicated to them. The right and duty of maintaining the shrines is a great honor, and it is passed along in certain clans according to very strict rules. Shinto helped to cement societal relationships in the villages where it was practiced.

In addition to the local *kami*, there are a number of common Shinto gods who are venerated throughout Japan. Among the most important is AMATERASU, the sun goddess who was associated with the YAMATO clan in early Japanese history.

The connection between the religion and government was extremely strong in ancient Japan. The emperor was believed to be descended from Amaterasu herself, and he presided over religious as well as government affairs and ceremonies.

Shinto's importance began to diminish with the arrival of BUDDHISM and the influence of China during the sixth century (see CHINESE INFLUENCE). But the new religion did not displace the old. Instead, Buddhism became intertwined with many of the older Shinto practices, and the two religions coexisted.

Shinto's influence and that of the emperor eroded during Japan's medieval period (1185–1868), but in 1871 it was reestablished as the state religion. The emperor's prestige was restored, and Shinto priests became government employees.

In the wake of World War II in the Pacific, (1941–45), the connection between government and religion was severed. The Japanese constitution prohibits the government from getting involved in religious matters. But Shinto shrines and beliefs permeate modern Japanese culture.

SHINTO GODS   The most important Shinto gods and goddesses include

- IZANAGI AND IZANAMI, the primordial, or first, gods, who created the world and many other gods.
- AMATERASU, the sun goddess and heaven's ruler. Her grandson is traditionally held to have become the first emperor of Japan.
- TSUKI-YOMI, Amaterasu's brother, the god of the moon.
- SUSANO-WO, the storm god and brother of Amaterasu. His feud with his sister caused him to be banished from heaven.
- NINIGI-NO-MIKOTO, the grandson of Amaterasu who was sent to rule the earth.
- TAKAMI-MUSUBI, one of Amaterasu's helpers
- UZUME, the dancing goddess who lured Amaterasu from the cave. She is usually called the goddess of the dawn.
- INARI, the god of rice.

SHI-RYO   Japanese ghosts. Like their Western counterparts, *shi-ryo* tend to visit the living only at night.

SHITATERA-HIME   The daughter of OKUNI-NUSHI, the SHINTO god of magic and medicine. Shitatera-Hime's husband is AME-NO-WAKAHIKO, whom the gods sent to check the state of things on earth.

SHITENNŌ (SHI TENNŌ)   See GUARDIAN KINGS.

SHITI DAMA   A wandering spirit or ghost in Japanese mythology. A shiti dama looks like a round or oval ball of fire in the distance.

SHODO SHONIN   Shodo Shonin was a devout priest who lived during the eighth century and is credited with founding a Buddhist temple at Nikkō in 766. He is also a legendary figure with fantastical stories attached to his name.

As he walked and prayed one day, he came to a large river that blocked his way. Shodo Shonin prayed that he might have a bridge to cross. Suddenly a giant appeared wearing snakes around his neck.

"Here!" shouted the giant, threateningly. He tossed down the snakes, which stretched across the raging waters. Shodo Shonin demonstrated his faith and courage by stepping onto the snakes as surely as if they were sturdy wooden planks and walking across to the other side of the river.

SHOGATSU-MATSURI   The annual New Year's festival of renewal and good fortune held January 1–3. During this time, many worshipers visit SHINTO SHRINES to venerate KAMI and ask for good fortune for the coming year. It is also a time when old home shrines are burned in special rituals. Arrows purchased for an offering at the shrines symbolize good luck for the coming year.

SHOGUN   The name for the military leaders or warlords who ruled during Japan's middle ages (1185–1868). The title was originally conferred upon military commanders or dictators by the imperial court. It was first used in the eighth century. Later the title became hereditary. The shogun passed his reign to his chosen heir—or at least attempted to do so in this period of great strife and conflict.

The three great Shogunates, or periods of military rule, are the Kamakura (1192–1333), established by Minamoto Yoritomo; the Ashikaga (1338–1573), established by Ashikaga Takauji; and the Tokugawa (1603–1867), established by Tokugawa Ieyasu in 1603.

The emperor remained technically the head of the country during all of this time. His divine status could not be entirely challenged, even by powerful warlords. In most matters concerning the military and practical government, however, he was a mere figurehead.

SHOJO   Shojo live at the bottom of the sea, according to Japanese myth and legend. In some ways they are similar to Western mermaids, though they are much more beneficial to humankind.

Shojo are masters of special medicines and other brews. Their wine has the power to kill a wicked person unless he or she repents immediately after drinking it. A good person who drinks the wine, however, tastes only incredible sweetness. *Shojo* have red or pinkish skin and red hair and wear seaweed skirts.

SHO KANNON   In Buddhist mythology, an incarnation of KANNON. Sho Kannon is the Japanese version of the Sanskrit Avalokitesvara. He is portrayed in art with one set of arms and often appears with a lotus, symbol of purity. Kannon serves and guides living things toward enlightenment and spares them suffering by his (or her) merciful nature.

SHOKI   A Buddhist god of the afterlife. Shoki opposes the ONI, or devils. He is said to be able to tame demons and is represented in art as an exorcist casting them out.

Scholars compare Shoki to the Chinese god Zhong Kui or Chung Kuei, whom he may be based on. The Chinese legends say that he was a physician and exorcist in China who was denied his rightful post by the emperor, who believed he looked too ugly. After he took his life on the steps of the imperial palace, the emperor felt sorry for barring him and ordered him buried in green robes, a royal honor. In gratitude, his spirit protected all emperors from devils.

Banners to Shoki are hung during TANGO NO SEKKU (the Boys' Festival) to keep evil spirits and bad luck away.

SHŌMON-JI   See ONMYŌ-JI.

SHORYOBUNI   "Soul ships." After BON (the Festival of the Dead), *shoryobuni* carry ghosts back to the spirit world. There are so many ghosts that the sea shines silvery white and their voices are heard in the winds.

Ships carrying mortals must steer clear of the *shoryobini*. Sailors unlucky enough to encounter them will be asked by the ghosts for pails. They must hand over bottomless pails or be sunk by the ghosts.

SHOTEN The Japanese version of Gaṇeśa, an Indian god of wisdom who has the head of an elephant. Gaṇeśa is worshiped by some sects of BUDDHISM, who see him as a mighty male god embracing a female Buddha-to-be. This is a symbolic reminder of the balance between male and female power and attributes. It also symbolizes how a follower must embrace and be embraced by the BUDDHA.

The god has great power. At times, he may make things difficult for a believer, giving him trials to overcome. At other times, he may remove these trials. A believer's struggle to overcome such difficulties helps him achieve enlightenment.

In the ancient Indian myths where Gaṇeśa originates, he is the son of Śiva. Śiva is the god of destruction or death, who works closely with his wife Śakti, the maternal goddess or goddess of life. They are often shown working together, and it is likely that some of Shoten's portrayals in art were influenced by Śiva.

SHŌTOKU (SHOTOKU TAISHI) (574–621) Prince Shōtoku played an important role in introducing BUDDHISM to Japan during the sixth century. Not only did he help win acceptance for Buddhism in Japan, but his emphasis on the *LOTUS SUTRA* influenced many people.

As a political leader, Shōtuko has few equals in world history. Shōtoku served as regent to the empress Suikō (554–628, reigned 593–628). Using China as a model, he reorganized the ruling bureaucracy and authored the Seventeen-Article Constitution, which set out the rules for Japanese government for years to come. He consolidated the emperor's power and was responsible for many public works such as irrigation systems that significantly improved the lives of the people.

Prince Shōtoku founded many Buddhist temples and greatly encouraged the spread of the religion. It is said that he wrote three commentaries on important Buddhist SUTRAS or scriptures, including the *LOTUS SUTRA*. After his death, many regarded him as a Buddhist saint.

Several Buddhist legends and myths were connected to him after his death. According to one, Shōtoku was able to speak and predict the future. Some Buddhists consider him a reincarnation of Siddhartha Gautama (known in Japan as Shāka), the historical founder of Buddhism. He is also seen as an early incarnation of the BOSATSU (future Buddha) MIRO.

Shōtoku holds a special place of honor in the Shin Buddhist sect. He is also seen as a patron of carpenters and craftsmen.

SHRINES Shrines are the focal point of many religious observances in SHINTO. They vary in size and style, from the personal family shrines usually found in every home to magnificent TEMPLES that are monumental works of architecture and art. No matter its size, each shrine holds a JINJA or *jingu*, an altar dedicated to the KAMI or deity venerated at the shrine.

Large public shrines include a *torii*, or gate, marking the passage from the outer world to the

Shinto shrines can be elaborate or very simple. Many had a practical aspect. This photo from the turn of the 20th century shows a shrine where believers would pray for the relief of a toothache. *(Library of Congress, Prints & Photographs Division [LC-USZ62-098861])*

world of gods. As he enters, a worshiper purifies his hands with pure water and then lightly rinses his mouth. This purifies the body so that it is ready to meet the *kami*.

There are usually two main parts of the shrine. The most important is the *honden*, or sanctuary. This is where the image of the *kami* is kept. Only priests enter this area of the temple.

Worshipers enter the *haiden*, the main area of the temple, where they make small offerings. They then alert the *kami* by ringing a bell or clapping twice. Bowing deeply, the believer then asks a favor of the *kami* or thanks the god for granting one. At the end of the prayer, the worshiper claps again.

Large shrines may include areas for rituals as well as booths or stalls selling good luck charms.

The miniature shrine found in homes is called a KAMIDANA, or "god shelf." Within this shrine's *honden* are the names of the family ancestors. Usually, the oldest member of the household looks after the *kamidana* daily, placing cups of sake and plates of rice as offerings for the ancestors venerated there. These family spirits are considered deities, just as the *kami* venerated at the larger shrines are.

It is usual in English to use *shrine* when referring to Shinto places of worship and *temple* when referring to those dedicated to BUDDHISM. However, the words can be used for both.

SIDDHARTHA, SIDDHARTHA GAUTAMA
See BUDDHA.

SILKWORM
The origin of silkworms and their threads is accounted for in a famous Japanese folktale. According to the tale, the father of a young woman was angry that she seemed to love the family's horse more than anything or anyone else in the world. So he killed the horse.

After the animal was dead, he took the skin off and hung it on a tree. The daughter found it and put it on as a kind of coat or dress. Magically she began to fly and was never seen again. A few days later, silkworms fell to earth from the sky into a mulberry tree. These were said to be the returning souls of the girl and her horse husband. Her father and mother carefully tended the worms, and the silk industry was born.

SOGA
The name of a powerful clan that advised early Japanese emperors in the Yamato family from 592 to 643. Historians compare Soga family members to today's prime ministers. In many instances these advisers had much more practical power than the emperor, though they relied on the emperor for legitimacy.

Soga daughters were married to members of the imperial dynasty, ensuring a close relationship. Some historians credit Soga officials with encouraging BUDDHISM in Japan for political reasons.

SOKO
One of the NIO, Buddhist deities who guard temple gates as well as monasteries.

SOKU-NO-KUMI
Another name for YOMI, the underworld. The words are usually translated into English as "the deep land."

SPIDERS
Spiders and "ground spiders" appear as enemies in the KOJIKI, a book on Japan's early history that is a storehouse of SHINTO myth. Scholars speculate that the original meaning was not monsters or arachnids, but people who were different from the YAMATO clan.

See also KUMO.

STARS
Unlike in some cultures, the stars do not appear to play an important role in early SHINTO myths. Chinese influence, however, brought a popular legend concerning the constellation known as WEAVER to Japan. The legend is connected to the festival of TANABATA.

In Buddhist mythology, the NIJUHACHIN BUSHU (constellations) are considered servants of KANNON, the BOSATSU of mercy.

SUGAWARA-NO-MICHIZANE (845–903)
A Japanese scholar, poet, and official who is regarded as the patron of scholarship in Japan. He fell out of favor with the emperor and was exiled in 901. Twenty years after his death, a number of calamities began to strike Japan. A number of Sugawara's old opponents suddenly died. The child of a Shinto priest had a vision that Sugawara had become the head of the thunder gods and was causing these disruptions. Japanese officials dedicated a

shrine to him in KYOTO, Kitano-jinja, to appease his spirit.

The process of appeasing or calming angry spirits, called *goryō*, with SHRINES was common throughout this period of Japan's history.

SUIJIN   A water spirit in Japanese mythology.

SUITENGU   The child god of the sea in SHINTO mythology.

SUKUNA-BIKONA (SUKU-NA-BIKO) Sukuna-Bikona is no taller than a dwarf, but this SHINTO god's powers include healing the sick and making plants grow. He is also honored as the god of hot springs. Kami-Musubi is his mother.

The stories of Sukuna-Bikona are often linked with the hero OKUNINUSHI. Sukuna-Bikona washed up on the shore near Okuninushi's castle one day. Curious, Okuninushi picked up the tiny dwarf in his hand. Angry, Sukuna-Bikona bit Okuninushi on the cheek. Okuninushi complained about this to the gods and discovered that Sukuna-Bikona was himself the son of a god who had fallen to earth. Okuninushi agreed to look after Sukuna-Bikona, but it was really the dwarf god who helped Okuninushi.

After much struggle, Okuninushi established himself as a ruler. Afterward, the little dwarf god simply disappeared.

SUN CULT   A sun cult is any religious group that worships the sun as their central or most important god. By this definition, the SHINTO pantheon—linked to the YAMATO family, the founding imperial dynasty of Japan—was the product of a sun cult. The Yamato clan's main goddess, AMATERASU, is a sun god, and the sun remains an important symbol of the country.

SUSANO-WO (SUSANO, SUSANOO, SUSAN-OTO, SUSA-NO-OR, SUSA-NO-WO) Susano-Wo, an important figure in SHINTO myth, was one of the gods born when Izanagi returned from YOUS, the land of the dead. He sprang from Izanagi's nose as the god purified himself from his long ordeal (see IZANAGI AND IZANAMI). His story is told in the Shinto CREATION MYTHS, which trace the beginning of the earth and Japan.

Susano-Wo is known as the "impetuous male," which is an apt description. At first, he was one of the most powerful gods. Izanagi gave him the sea to rule over, but Susano-Wo was not satisfied. His sister AMATERASU had been given the sun and his brother the moon. Angry, he vowed to join his mother Izanami in the underworld. Izanagi banished Susano-Wo as punishment for his ingratitude.

Leaving peacefully would have been against Susano-Wo's stormy nature. Jealous of his sister, he challenged Amaterasu to a contest. Whoever could create more gods, he said, would be the winner.

Amaterasu broke her brother's sword into three pieces. Then she ate it and spit out the pieces. Three goddesses formed from the mist.

Susano-Wo took his sister's beads and cracked them with his teeth. Five male gods appeared.

He declared himself the winner.

Amaterasu said no. Since the gods had come from her jewels, obviously she was stronger. His sword had yielded only three gods, and they were female.

Susano-Wo stormed so fiercely that Amaterasu retreated to a cave, bringing great destruction to the earth. In the meantime, the other gods grew angry at Susano-Wo and weary of his behavior. They finally stripped him of his possessions—and even his beard and fingernails. He was barred from heaven.

Other myths and legends tell of what happened to Susano-Wo after he was barred from heaven. In some of these stories Susano-Wo is a hero rather than a testy or troublesome villain. These two personalities may be the result of different local traditions. It is also said that when he was being bad, Susano-Wo followed his wicked soul, or Ara-mi-tama; when he was good, he followed his Nigi-mi-tama, or good soul.

In one story, Susano-Wo became angry with UKE-MOCHI, the food goddess, when she disgusted him by pulling food from her rectum, nose, and mouth. But when he killed her, rice and other grains and vegetables sprouted from her body, bringing these vital crops to the world. (Similar legends have the moon god TSUKIYOMI killing Ukemochi or INARI.)

Susano-Wo used magic to fight the eight-headed snake Koshi in a terrible battle, winning his wife and a sword called KUSANAGI-NO-TSURUGI ("The Grass Cutter" or "Grass-Cutting Sword"). Here is the story:

One day after he had come to earth Susano-Wo fell in love with a beautiful girl. But her parents told him that her seven sisters had been killed by a fierce monster, who was returning to kill this girl as well. Susano-Wo said that he would save her—if he could marry her. When her parents agreed, Susano-Wo turned the girl into a comb and tucked her safely into his hair. The snake soon appeared but was enticed by eight tubs of wine, which he quickly drank. After the monster fell asleep, Susano-Wo lopped off his many heads, winning the girl and finding Kusanagi in its tail.

Other legends tell of Susano-Wo conquering KOREA and stopping a devastating attack of the plague. At some point, he may have become confused with Gozu-Tennō, a foreign god who is shown with an ox head and said to be the god of plagues.

SUTRA   A sacred BUDDHIST text. Sutras contain or are thought to contain BUDDHA's words. They range in size and intent. Some are short sayings; others are long commentaries on difficult points. The most important sutra in Japanese BUDDHISM is the *LOTUS SUTRA*.

SWORD   See AMA-NO-MURAKAMO-NO-TSURUGI.

T

TAIRA The Taira clan fought with the MINAMOTO clan to rule over Japan during the 12th century. This was during Japan's great feudal period, and stories and tales of battles from those days, such as those in the epic *Tale of* HEIKE, remain popular today. (See FEUDALISM IN JAPAN.) The Taira were also known as the Heike.

One of the most famous stories concerns the escape in 1160 of the emperor from Kyoto after the Minamoto leaders rebelled and tried to take over. Disguising himself as a woman, the emperor fled to a Taira stronghold. The clan returned with the emperor and routed the rebels.

The conflict between the two clans ended in the GEMPEI WAR (1180–85). The Taira lost the war and their power declined, although they continued to play an important role in Japan.

TAISHAKU The Japanese equivalent of Indra, an important Hindu god. In Buddhist mythology, Taishaku lives in Tuşita Heaven, one of the many Buddhist HEAVENS. Taishaku is mentioned in the *Tale of the* HEIKE.

TAKAMAGAHARA HEAVEN, or the realm of the gods in SHINTO. The word itself means "the higher heavenly plain." Takamagahara is connected to the earth by the floating bridge, or AMA-NO-UKI-HASHI.

TAKAMI-MUSUBI Takami-Musubi is the creator god of SHINTO. He rules the world with the sun goddess AMATERASU, who is his wife, and is the grandfather of NINIGI-NO-MIKOTO, the first emperor of Japan.

Though his place is very important, Takami-Musubi does not receive as much mention as Amaterasu or their descendants in the early mythic texts that have come down to us.

TAKARA-BUNE The ship used by the SHICHI FUJUKIN, the seven gods of good luck or happiness. Each New Year's Eve they sail to shore carrying several treasures: the purse that never empties, the hat that makes its wearer invisible, the lucky coat, the wealth hammer or MALLET, the rat that chases ghosts, the magic key, and the full bag of RICE.

According to Japanese folklore, a child who puts a picture of the *Takara-Bune* under his pillow will have happy dreams.

TAKE-MIAZUCHI (TAKE-MIA-ZUCHI, TAKEMIKADZUCHI) A SHINTO thunder god. The other gods sent Take-Miazuchi to subdue the province of IZUMO. Take-Miazuchi also consulted with AMATERASU when Emperor JIMMU was in trouble and sent the emperor a magic sword to slay his enemies.

TAKI-TSU-HIKO A SHINTO god of rain.

TALE OF THE GENJI See GENJI, TALE OF THE.

TAMON-TEN (TAMON) Another name for BISHAMON.

TANABATA Held each July 7, Tanabata, or the Weaver's Festival, is based on a tale thought to have originated in China in ancient days. The name of the festival is a reference to the seventh night of the seventh moon. It is sometimes compared to Valentine's Day because it celebrates a romantic story, which is known as "WEAVER AND COWHERD."

According to the tale, the weaver can meet her lover only once a year. The details of the story match the movement of the stars Westerners call Vega and Altair, which come together in the Milky Way once a year. (Vega is the Weaver. Altair is also known as the Ox Driver.) This meeting is celebrated with love poems and special exhibitions of girls' arts and crafts at school.

TANGO NO SEKKU The Boys' Festival, an annual event in Japan. Tango no sekku, held each May 5, is a celebration traditionally honoring young Japanese boys, now often celebrating all children.

A counterpart to HINAMATSURI (The Girls' Festival), the Boys' Festival reminds children of the great deeds done by legendary and mythic heroes as well as their own ancestors and historic figures. Dolls and weapons symbolizing these legends are displayed, and it is common to fly a CARP flag or kite in the garden. The carp is a symbol of strength and an inspiration for his hard fight against the current when he grows of mating age.

The *Tale of the* HEIKE, written during Japan's feudal age, mentions this festival because of its importance then in warding off spring diseases. It was called "Sweet Flag" because the leaves of sweet flag, also known as calamus, were worn, hung in rooms, and used in ceremonies to ward off disease.

TAOISM (DAOISM, TAO-TE CHING) Taoism is an ancient combination of religion, philosophy, and folk beliefs, including ritual healing. It began more than 2,000 years ago in China.

According to its teaching, the wise person must strive to put him- or herself at one with the Tao or "Way." The Tao is beyond easy definition. It is the spirit and animating force that underlies all things in the universe. A Taoist accepts the world as it is, adopting an easygoing attitude or perhaps withdrawing without trying to change it, since the world is not the most important reality.

Taoism makes great use of magic and mystical or unworldly experiences. Some Tao teachers experience ecstasies, trancelike states where they learn truths. Historically, mysticism was an important part of the Taoism, though from time to time the purely philosophical elements have been emphasized.

The Chinese philosopher Lao-tzu, credited with writing the *Tao-te Ching* (*The Book of the Way* is one translation), is traditionally said to be the founder of Taoism. But whether Lao-tzu actually existed and whether Taoism had already been established are matters of considerable debate among scholars.

Taoism's ideas had a direct and subtle influence on Buddhism, both in China and Japan. It also came to Japan directly through teachers and folk practitioners called ONMYO-JI. These fortune-tellers were often employed to study omens and advise when the time might be good for different activities, such as getting married.

TATSUTA-HIKO AND TATSUTA-HIME The SHINTO god and goddess of the wind venerated near Tatsuta. They bring good harvests and are also connected with the coming of autumn.

TAWARA-TODA Another name for HIDESATO, a legendary hero who helped the DRAGON KING. The name means "bag of rice that never needs to be refilled."

TEA Tea is an important drink throughout much of Asia, including Japan. It arrived in Japan from China, probably around 800. Japanese farmers began growing it no later than the 12th century.

The beverage's connection to BUDDHISM is celebrated in a legend that claims it was discovered by a MONK named Bodhidharma in India. According to the legend, the monk nearly fell asleep several times during his meditation, which would have ruined his proper preparation for becoming a BUDDHA. To keep his eyes from closing, he cut off his eyelids and threw them on the ground. Tea bushes grew where they fell.

TEA CEREMONY (CHADO, CHANOYU) The ritual of the tea ceremony began in Japan during the Muromachi period (1336–1573). It celebrates friendship as well as one's link with history, ancestors, and the spirit of Japan.

Ostensibly, the tea ceremony seems like a very simple event. A few friends, sometimes only one, come to drink TEA. They are greeted by their host carefully but simply, then led to a small building or pavilion in a garden. When they are seated, there they might see a single flower on a table, or be shown a lone vase or other art object. A meal and then the tea itself will be served very slowly, according to a ritual that emphasizes the art and grace of every move-

Tea is an important part of Asian cultures, and in Japan its importance goes far beyond its use as a beverage. Here a teakettle has a mythological scene. (*Christopher Dresser,* Japan: Its Architecture, Art, and Art Manufactures, *1882)*

ment. In modern tea ceremonies, young women may serve the tea.

The tea ceremony is a study in subtlety and understatement, with an emphasis on contemplation. Each step in the ceremony follows a careful plan, and even the utensils and teapot are set by ritual. The ceremony was developed into an art form by ZEN masters during the 15th century. It is still practiced today throughout Japan and the world.

TEMPLES Like Christian churches in the West, temples are the center of religious activity in BUDDHISM.

Besides religious activities, such as funeral rites, many temples provide important community services, including preschool. Many temples in rural Japan include cemeteries. A number of very old temples are now visited by tourists because of their artistic and historical interest, as well as for religious reasons.

Temples vary according to sect and location, but their precincts or grounds usually include several buildings made entirely of wood. The most important is the pagoda, which houses relics and scriptures sacred to the sect. The *butsudan* or *kondo* houses statues of deities. SUTRAS, the important teachings or scriptures of Buddhism, are read in the *hotto* or *kodo*. Large temples can also include administrative buildings, quarters for monks and nuns, and special halls for visitors. The main entrance at the temple gate is called a *sammon*, and every temple includes hanging bells, called *tsurigane* or *bonsho*, struck with a large wooden mallet to produce a distinctive ring. In many temples, especially those related to ZEN Buddhism, gardens add an important perspective to religious meditation.

Among the countless temples in Japan, one of the most famous is Hōryūji in Nara, built by Prince SHŌTOKU (573–621). Said to have been built in 585, the original temple burned down in 670 but was quickly reconstructed. It is the oldest monastic compound in Japan. Also in Nara is Tōdaiji, built by Emperor Shōmu (701–756). This temple was razed during the medieval period but was then restored. Among its many great works of art and devotion it features a massive statue of Buddha. The Byōdōin at Uji was once a mansion but was converted in 1053 to a temple meant to evoke the paradise promised to believers of the Pure Land sect (see PURE LAND BUDDHISM). It is a beautiful example of Heian architecture. Among the many historic temples in and around Kyoto are Nanzen, one of the oldest centers of Zen Buddhism in the country; Kiyomizu-dera, said to have been built from the timbers of the old imperial palace in Nagaoka and one of the oldest surviving structures in the city; Sanjūsangendō, where a massive statue of KANNON and 1,001 gilded images attract hundreds of visitors a day; Daitoku, a Zen temple that covers 27 acres; Kinkaku, which contains the glittering Golden Pavilion (the original was destroyed in 1950 but rebuilt five years later); and Saihō, whose moss gardens are a unique point of devotion for many.

It is common in English to call Shinto religious buildings as well as altars *shrines*, and use *temples* only when referring to sacred Buddhist sites. However, the words are often interchanged.

Because SHINTO and BUDDHISM are closely connected in Japan, elements connected with either religion may be found in the other. Large complexes may contain temples and shrines next to each other.

TEN Another name for heaven or paradise. The word can also refer to the sky or god.

TENDAI A popular sect of Japanese BUDDHISM known for its acceptance of meditation and *taimitsu*, or esoteric practices. These practices include elaborate rituals and magic.

In 805 the MONK Saicho returned from a visit to China, where he had studied the *LOTUS SUTRA* with monks on Mount Tendai. This Buddhist text holds that BUDDHA's divine nature extends all through the universe, in life and even in inanimate objects such as rocks and stones. It can be experienced by everyone with the help of *BOSATSU*, or Buddhas to be, as well as ritual and magic.

Tendai had an enormous influence on Japanese Buddhism. According to this teaching, it was possible to view SHINTO deities, or *KAMI*, as manifestations of these divine beings. This flexibility made it possible for Buddhist myths to coexist and even merge with earlier Shinto beliefs.

TENGU *Tengu* are devil spirits in Japanese legends and folktales. These bogeymen live in the forests and on mountains, where they torment children.

A *tengu* uses a wild boar as transportation in this early Japanese woodcut, based on a drawing by Kokan. *(Collected by William Anderson in* Japanese Wood Engravings, *1908)*

Tengu have long noses and beaks on their ugly faces, as well as wings that allow them to fly. Some call them birdmen because of these qualities. In some cases they can do magic or have enchanted items; one popular folktale tells of a *tengu* coat that makes its owner invisible. In some tales they carry off children and novice Buddhist MONKS.

Not all the spirits are evil, and they can help people. For example, the legendary hero Tameto was helped by *tengu*, who saved him from the jaws of a monster fish. Tengu also are said to guard the MIKOSHI (portable shrines) during the annual festival known as a MATSURI.

TENJIN Kitano Tenjin is the Japanese *KAMI*, or SHINTO deity, of learning and calligraphy.

Tenjin is linked to the ninth-century scholar and nobleman SUGAWARA-NO-MICHIZANE, a historical figure. Michizane was banished by political rivals. After his death, KYOTO (then called Heian) suffered many calamities. At the time, people believed these were caused by Michizane's unhappy spirit. The Kitano SHRINE was built in his honor, satisfying the ghost, whose name was venerated as Tenjin, or "heavenly person." Pleased, Tenjin extended his assistance to students and scholars. He still helps those who call on him for help learning difficult lessons. Tenjin shrines are found throughout Japan.

TENNIN *(TENSHI)* Spirits taking human form, comparable to an angel in Western mythologies. Devout Buddhists may climb mountains searching for religious enlightenment. On the pilgrimage, a spirit may appear as a beautiful person, or *tennin*. The appearance of the *tennin* is a great blessing.

TENRIKYO One of 13 new SHINTO sects recognized by the Japanese government in 1912, Tenrikyo was started by Mika Nakayama (1798–1887) in 1836. Known as "Heavenly Truth," the religion harks back to the roots of Shinto, though it is considered by scholars a "NEW RELIGION" to distinguish it from traditional Shinto and BUDDHISM. It is an important religion in Japan today and has more than 2 million members.

Mika Nakayama, a farm woman, said she was possessed by Ten-taishōgun, the Great General of Heaven, who chose her to spread the truth about heaven and humans' place in the universe. According to Ten-taishōgun, there are only 10 *KAMI*: himself and nine lesser gods. Mika Nakayama wrote a poem called "Ofudesaki" setting out her beliefs.

THERĀVADA BUDDHISM The conservative branch of BUDDHISM, which stands in contrast to MAHĀYĀNA. Known as the "Way of the Elders," the Therāvada schools hold that ENLIGHTENMENT can be achieved only by the means outlined in the conservative texts. In general, the Therāvada Buddhists do not consider it possible to achieve enlightenment without becoming a MONK.

Mahāyāna Buddhism had a large influence in Japan. Therāvada did not.

THREE TREASURES The *sanshu no jingi*, or "three sacred treasures," given by the sun goddess AMATERASU to her grandson NINIGI-NO-MIKOTO when she sent him to rule the earth. They are the sword (AMA-NO-MURAKUMO-NO-TSURUGI), the MIRROR (YATA NO KAGAMI), and the string of jewels (YASAKANI NO MAGATAMA).

THUNDER A frequent subject of mythological interest, thunder is mentioned in connection with several different Japanese deities.

In the SHINTO CREATION MYTH, thunder gods guard Izanami in the underworld, YOMI, after her death (see IZANAGI AND IZANAMI). Mythologists have suggested that these gods are actually connected with the rumblings of an earthquake or volcanic activity, which would be something more likely to be associated with the underworld than actual thunder.

The god SUSANO-WO is often connected with storms and thunder. So is the god TAKE-MIAZUCHI, who conquered the troublesome IZUMO region. And AJI-SUKI-TAKA-HIKONE is connected with a story that tired parents might still tell their children at bedtime: When the little thunder god was born, he cried so badly that his parents carried him up and down the heavenly ladder, hoping to get him to fall asleep.

TIDE JEWELS The jewels with which RYUJIN, the SHINTO god of the sea, regulates the tides. According to legend, Ryujin gave the jewels to Empress JINGŌ to help her invade KOREA. As Jingō's ships approached the Korean fleet, she threw the low tide jewel into the water. The tide went out and the Korean ships were stranded on the sand. As soon as the Korean sailors jumped out to escape, Jingō threw the high tide jewel into the water. They were drowned as the water quickly rose, and Jingō won her battle.

TOKOYO The heroine of a Japanese legend demonstrating a daughter's love and duty toward her father. Tokoyo's father was a SAMURAI named Oribe Shima. Though brave, the samurai displeased his emperor and was banished from the kingdom.

Tokoyo missed her father and eventually decided to look for him. She went to Akasaki and found some fishermen, hoping to persuade them to row her to the Oki Islands. But they refused, since it was against the law to take anyone to the exiles there.

Tokoyo took a boat herself. When she arrived, she was warned not to say her father's name, since looking for him was forbidden. Instead, she wandered around the island, looking and listening for clues.

Her search brought her to a Buddhist TEMPLE. After praying there, Tokoyo saw a Buddhist priest leading a crying girl away. She followed as they walked to a cliff. Tokoyo barely managed to stop the priest from throwing the girl into the waves.

The priest explained sadly that the sacrifice was necessary. The god YOFUNE-NUSHI demanded a young maiden each year, or he would send storms to drown the local fisherman.

Tokoyo told the priest she would go in the girl's place. The loss of her father had destroyed her desire to live, she said.

But Tokoyo was not really ready to die—or at least, she was not prepared to do so without a fight. With a dagger in her teeth and prayers to BUDDHA, she jumped into the ocean. She would kill Yofune-Nushi and end his terror.

At the bottom of the sea sat the entrance to a large cave. Tokoyo entered. There she found a statue of the emperor who had banished her father. At first she wanted to hack it to pieces. But then she decided she would take it back to the island with her.

As she began to leave, a serpent came to stop her. But Tokoyo blinded the monster, then killed it. She returned to land, where the surprised Buddhist

priest heard the story and proclaimed that she was a hero. When the emperor heard the story, he realized that he had been freed from an evil spell. Oribe Shima was reunited with his daughter, and the two returned home.

TOKUTARO-SAN The Tokutaro-San is a doll the size of a real two-year-old. Some believe that such dolls have magic powers and can cry and even run away. Proper care of a Tokutaro-San will bring a family good luck. Such care includes changing their clothes and keeping them looking new.

A Tokutaro-San is passed from generation to generation. The dolls are believed responsible for children's being born healthy. Breaking the doll is considered very bad luck. Dolls that have grown too worn or broken must be laid under an *enoki* tree (a nettle tree) to be "buried" properly.

A Tokutaro-San is a boy doll. The female doll is called an Otoku-San.

TOKYO Today one of the largest and most important cities in the world, Tokyo was a small fishing village in eastern Japan until the Tokugawa Shogunate, or military government (1603–1867), when it became the capital of the country. Known then as EDO, the city increased tremendously in size, quickly becoming the biggest city in Japan. At the same time, KYOTO remained the emperor's home. When the emperor's importance as head of the government was reinstated with the MEIJI Restoration (1868), the imperial residence moved to Tokyo.

TOKYO-NO-KUNI Tokyo-no-Kuni is the "eternal country"; in other words, paradise or the spirit world.

TONGUE-CUT SPARROW The name in English of a popular Japanese folktale that exists in many versions. The tale illustrates the Buddhist ideas that good works are rewarded and jealousy is punished. Following is the basic story, including an ending that reinforces the Buddhist moral:

A woodcutter was out one day feeding the birds near his house when he heard the cry of a sparrow. The bird had hurt its legs. Taking pity on it, he picked it up and brought it home to care for it.

The man's wife objected. She claimed that they did not have enough food even for a tiny bird. True, they were poor, but mostly she complaining simply because she was a cross and disagreeable woman.

Soon, the sparrow began to feel better. It loved the woodcutter very much and would ride on his shoulder all day singing. One day, the sparrow stayed home while the man went out to work. The woodcutter's wife had left out some rice paste. The bird found it and ate it.

The wife was so furious she grabbed the bird. She vowed to punish it. With a sharp knife she slit the sparrow's tongue so that it could no longer sing. The sparrow flew away.

When the woodcutter came home, he asked where the bird was. His wife told him the story angrily. Saddened, he went in search of the poor little bird. Some sparrows outside heard him calling. They came down and led him through the woods to a special house far away. The sparrow was actually the daughter of the Sparrow King. The man joined them for a great feast. Afterward he was tempted to stay, but he decided he must go home to see his wife.

As a gift, the Sparrow King offered him the choice of two baskets—one large, one small. Being a humble man without great needs, the woodcutter chose the smaller basket, then went home.

His wife was as nasty as ever when he returned—until he opened the basket. Inside were silks and jewels. But when the woodcutter told his wife how he had chosen between the two baskets, she raged.

"We should be twice as rich," she claimed. And then she went herself to find the sparrows' home.

When she arrived, she insulted the family with her brusque ways. But the Sparrow King gave her a choice of baskets even so. She took the larger, then hurried home.

When she opened the basket, evil demons tried to carry her off to hell. It was only by repenting her evil and calling to BUDDHA that she was saved.

TOYOTAMA   According to SHINTO myth, Toyotama was the daughter of the sea god. She fell in love with HIKOHOHODEMI, and they lived happily beneath the sea for many years.

When the pair returned to land, Toyotama became pregnant. She warned Hikohohodemi that he must not watch her give birth. He agreed and she went into a hut to have their child. But Hikohohodemi did not keep his promise. He peeked through a crack in the hut and watched her turn into a sea DRAGON. After giving birth, Toyotama returned to the sea. Her sister, Tamayori-Hime, came from the ocean to look after the child. When the boy grew into a man, he married Tamayori-Hime. Their son had two names, Toyo-Mike-Nu and Kamu-Yamato-Iware-Hiko. According to legend, this son became JIMMU TENNŌ, the first emperor of Japan.

Toyotama is also known as Otohime.

TOYOTOMI HIDEYOSHI   See HIDEYOSHI.

TOYO-UKE-BIME   A SHINTO goddess of earth, food, and farming.

TOYOUKE-OMIKAMI   A SHINTO goddess of grain. Her shrine, or *geku*, is served by a priestess, known as a *saigu*.

TSUKIYOMI (TSUKI-YUMI)   The SHINTO god of the Moon. He is the brother of AMATERASU, the sun goddess, and SUSANO-WO, the storm god. Tsukiyomi was born from Izanagi's right eye after Izanagi cleansed himself following his trip to YOMI, the underworld (see IZANAGI AND IZANAMI).

As god of the Moon, Tsukiyomi rules the night. In some myths, he is said to have killed UKEMOCHI (in some versions, INARI), the Shinto goddess of food. This act brought RICE and other important foods to earth.

According to these myths, Tsukiyomi asked the goddess for food. She responded by pulling it from her anus, mouth, and nose. Tsukiyomi was insulted and killed her. From her body sprang rice and other plants.

Amaterasu was angered by her brother's violence and vowed never to see him again. That is why the Sun and Moon rise and set separately.

Other versions of this story say that SUSANO-WO killed Ukemochi.

TSUKIYOMO   A female version of TSUKIYOMI. This form is used when the moon god is referred to as a female.

TSUYU According to Japanese legend, Tsuyu fell in love with a SAMURAI warrior and waited for him to return from battle. The samurai, meanwhile, heard that Tsuyu had died. Though this was wrong, he believed it. Tsuyu pined away for her lover, then finally died out of grief. She floated through the world as a ghost until she found her samurai's house. The next morning, the samurai was found dead in bed—clutching Tsuyu's skeleton.

TUMULUS PERIOD   See KOFUN PERIOD.

U

UBA The pine tree spirit, Uba symbolizes the best parts of contented married life in Japanese legend. Her name can be translated as "old woman" or "old wet nurse," a revered motherly figure. An old woman, she lives with her husband, Jo, whose name means "love."

UGA-JIN Uga-Jin is an ancient serpent god of the sea in Japanese myth. Scholars suggest the god symbolizes fertility.

UGA-NO-MITAMA A SHINTO goddess of agriculture. She is venerated at a shrine near Kyoto, where the presence of foxes suggests a connection to Inari, the Shinto god of rice. Her male counterpart is Uka-no-Mikoto, the *kami* of grains.

UJIGAMI According to Shinto beliefs, every family is protected and helped by ujigami, or ancestral gods, who have generally helped the family from generation to generation. These "house gods" are honored at small shrines (KAMIDANA) in homes. Among the favors they traditionally grant are predictions about illnesses.

UKEMOCHI (UKE-MOCHI) A SHINTO god, Ukemochi symbolizes food and fertility. Tsukiyomi, the moon god, met her one day and asked for food. Ukemochi vomited a great deal of food, then produced more from her nose and anus. Offended, Tsukiyomi killed her, and from her body sprang animals and a wide variety of vegetables such as rice and beans, millet, wheat, and soybeans. A cow and horse also appeared.

In some versions of this myth, Ukemochi's killer is the storm god SUSANO-WO. And in others, INARI, the rice god/goddess, is killed.

UKIYO-E *Ukiyo-e* means "pictures of the floating world." The name includes a reference to what today we might call the X-rated or red-light district of cities. Many early works were erotic, but the art form quickly expanded to include a wide range of topics. Everyday life, KABUKI actors, historical events, and myth were common topics.

Typical *ukiyo-e* began as ink drawings, which were then carved into woodblocks by craftsmen and printed. Ten to 16 blocks, each printing a different color or shade, might be used to make a typical print. The art work often appeared in books and albums as well as stand-alone prints.

Begun around 1600 and reaching its peak in the 1800s, the *ukiyo-e* movement help acquaint many people in the West with a variety of features of Japanese life, including popular myths and legends. Today, the colorful prints are highly prized in the United States and Europe as well as Japan.

UNDERWORLD See YOMI.

URASHIMA TARO The story of Urashima is often compared to the American story of Rip Van Winkle, though the ancient Japanese mythological hero meets a much harder fate. Urashima was fishing one day when he caught a large tortoise in his net. Feeling sorry for it, he cut the tortoise loose, freeing it to return to the sea. But the creature was actually one of the daughters of RYUJIN, the SHINTO god of the sea. She spoke to Urashima, inviting him to come to RYUGU, the sea god's palace. Not completely believing he was speaking to a tortoise, he agreed to go.

As he swam he saw a vast and beautiful palace made of sea shells, coral, and pearls. When they arrived at the palace, the tortoise changed into a beautiful girl. Urashima fell in love with her, and they

Urashima was warned not to open the box, but he could not keep himself from doing so. *(From Yei Theodora Ozaki,* Japanese Fairy Tales, *1903)*

were soon married. But after four years he felt homesick, and asked to go home to see his parents. Urashima's wife gave him a box with magical powers that would allow him to return to her when he wanted—but only if it remained closed.

Back on land, Urashima found that much had changed. His parents were long gone. Finally in confused desperation, he asked an old man if he had known Urashima.

Urashima, said the old man, drowned in the sea 400 years ago.

Urashima, though he had hardly aged at all, had been away for 400 years. His parents and all his friends were long dead. Stunned, he opened the box,

forgetting his wife's warning not to. Instantly, he aged and disappeared into dust.

USHIWAKA   Another name for YORISUNE.

UWIBAMI   Uwibami is one of many monstrous serpents appearing in Japanese myths and legends. It was said to be so large it could swallow a man and horse whole. After it terrorized many people, the hero Yegara-no-Heida killed it.

UZUME (USUME, AME-NO-UZUME)   Uzume is the "whirling," dancing SHINTO goddess of the dawn. She is known as the goddess of the dawn and laughter, and her best-known tale in the SHINTO CREATION MYTH involves both.

When AMATERASU hid herself away in a cave after the earth was created, the world was covered in darkness and cold. Uzume came and danced outside of the cave. As Uzume continued to dance, she threw off all her clothes. The other gods laughed and applauded. Finally Amaterasu came out to see what was going on. Her return brought the sunshine back to the dark earth, and life returned.

Later, when Amaterasu sent her grandson NINIGI-NO-MIKOTO to rule the earth, the guardian of AMA-NO-UKI-HASHI, the Floating Bridge, blocked his path. Uzume danced once more, distracting the god with her movements. SARVTAHIKO OHAKAMI, the guardian of the Floating Bridge, was so impressed by her dances that he asked her to marry him. She did, and lived with him at the bridge, which connects heaven and earth.

Uzume's dances, called *ama-no-uzume,* are included in many folk rites. The KAGURA, for example, are dances to wake the dead. Other dances celebrate the planting of seeds and the seasons.

VAIROCANA The Sanskrit name for DAINICHI.

VOLCANOES Like many other natural features, volcanoes were considered gods in SHINTO mythology. The most famous example is FUJI-SAN, or Mount Fuji. Climbing the mountains is considered a pilgrimage and an act of homage to the *KAMI* that inhabit it.

The majestic, snow-covered peak now seems harmless from the distance, but Fuji has simmered for 10,000 years. The last violent eruption came in the early 18th century, and scientists say that a fresh eruption there could impact ecosystems across the world for years. Eruptions at any of the 86 active volcanoes in Japan could disrupt the lives of millions of people, and a major eruption could have worldwide implications.

Fuji-san, or Mount Fuji, as the mountain is known in the West, is a potent symbol of Japan. It is also a volcano, which last erupted in the 18th century. *(From Isabell L. Bird,* Unbeaten Tracks in Japan, *1880)*

WAKA A Japanese poem. Poems often use themes from myth and legend, or make reference to them.

The classic form of *waka* is the *tanka*, or short poem, which consists of five lines with 31 syllables arranged in an alternating pattern: five-seven-five-seven-seven. Written in KANA, the form flourished from about the sixth century, becoming dominant in the ninth. Linked verse, known as *renga*, became popular in the 14th century. It gradually gave way to the HAIKU around the 17th century. Poets seeking to return to the roots of Japanese literature and culture restored the *waka* style around the turn of the 20th century. Today, the term *tanka* is generally reserved for poetry written in the modern era, and *waka* refers to classical works.

WAKAHIRU-ME The goddess of the rising sun. In the Shinto creation myths, Wakahiru is the younger sister of AMATERASU. She was with her sister when the impetuous god SUSANO-WO threw the flayed horse into Amaterasu's weaving hell.

WATANABE A faithful companion of the legendary hero RAIKO, Watanabe is the hero of a popular legend about a fight with an ONI at the Gate of RASHŌMON, the southern gate of the city of Nara.

Hearing that an *oni* was terrorizing people there, Watanabe set out to find it. But there was nothing by the gate when he arrived. He wrote his name on a piece of paper and left it there as proof that he had come. Then he turned to go.

Something grabbed him from behind and threw him down. Realizing it was an *oni*, the SAMURAI slashed at his captor. The *oni* tried to frighten him with its terrible face, but Watanabe was too brave. Finally, the monster had enough of the battle and fled. Watanabe gave chase, but could not catch him.

The brave Watanabe challenged and defeated a menacing *oni* at the Gate of Rashōmon. The monster fled, leaving behind its severed arm. *(From Yei Theodora Ozaki,* Japanese Fairy Tales, *1903)*

Back at the gate, he found the *oni*'s arm. This was quite a prize. He took it home as a trophy, locking it away.

One day an old woman came and knocked on his door. She claimed to be his old nurse and begged one favor: to see the arm of the *oni* before she died.

Watanabe said no. He was afraid that the arm might harm her somehow. But after a while, Watanabe finally gave in. He allowed the nurse to look at the arm. The nurse grabbed it and put it on, instantly changing back into the *oni*.

Watanabe grabbed his sword but the *oni* managed to get away. Still, it was so frightened of the samurai that it never harmed anyone again.

WATA-TSU-MI   A Japanese sea god.

WATERIGAWA   See SANZU NO KAWA.

WEAVER AND COWHERD   A variation of the story Westerners call Vega and Altair, two constellations that come together in the Milky Way once a year. (Vega is the Weaver. Altair is also known as the ox driver.) The legend explains the movement of the STARS, and mythology experts believe it originated in China. According to the story, the weaver can meet her lover only once a year, just as the stars do. The story is connected with the festival of TANABATA.

In one of the many versions of the tale, the maiden Tanabata spent her days weaving garments for her father, the august God of the Firmament (heavens). One day she saw a handsome young man named Hiko-boshi leading an ox in the fields. They fell in love.

Tanabata's father liked Hikoboshi and agreed to the match, but things did not go well. The girl neglected her duties at the loom. Even worse, Hiko-boshi let his ox wander around the High Plain of Heaven, upsetting others. The God of the Firmament became extremely angry and separated the lovers by the Celestial River. Only on the seventh night of the seventh month could they meet—crossing a bridge formed by a mass of birds.

WEAVING   The art of weaving and cloth making was an important one in Japan, just as it was in many ancient societies. One sign of its importance is the fact that AMATERASU is seen weaving in the SHINTO CREATION MYTHS. According to Shinto myths, Amaterasu and her ladies-in-waiting were creating cloths in her weaving hall when the sea god or storm god SUSANA-WO threw a flayed horse into her chamber. This upset her so much that she fled into a dark cave.

Today, most cloth is made by machines, but handmade silk and other materials are greatly prized in Japan as elsewhere around the world. Clothes, wall hangings, and other items often use symbols and pictures from myth and legend as part of their design.

WIND GODS   The principal SHINTO wind gods are SHINA-TSU-HIKO and his wife, SHINE-TO-BE. Together, they fill the space between the earth and heaven. Other Shinto wind gods include HAYA-JI, the god of the whirl-wind, and TATSUTA-HIKO and TATSUTA-HIME, who bring good harvests in the region near Tatsuta.

WOMEN   For much of Japan's recorded history, women were largely confined to subservient social roles. However, exceptions to this general rule are noted in both myth and legend. For example, in the SHINTO CREATION MYTH, the most important deity in heaven is AMATERASU, the sun goddess. Many historians and anthropologists believe these references indicate that early Japanese culture had matriarchal clan structures and that women played an important role in leading society.

Female SHAMANS played an important role in ancient Japan in the observance of religious rites and in curing illnesses. During the Japanese middle ages, women were often drawn into battle, defending towns in the local wars that raged across the country. Martial arts traditions in both Japan and the rest of the West hark back to this time, training women with the paginate, a long blade mounted on a five- to eight-foot shaft, which can be wielded with deadly force.

Three great women warriors are among the most celebrated heroes in Japanese history and legend: Empress JINGŌ, Tomoe Gozen, and Han Gaku or Hangaku, also called Itagki. While tales told about them sometimes contain fantastical elements, all were real people.

Although women heroes were honored, men did not necessarily accept them readily or as full equals. Han Gaku's story illustrates this fact: Gaku was a real woman who lived around 1200 in the province of Echigo (now Nigata). She fought against the Kamakura Shogunate (see KAMAKURA PERIOD) but eventually lost. According to legend, Kamakura was going to execute her but one of his warriors, impressed by her beauty and spirit, saved her by making her his wife.

AINU legends include another story about dominating a strong woman, Poi-Soya-Un-Mat. The humorous story is often compared to Shakespeare's play *The Taming of a Shrew*. Poi-Soya-Un-Mat dresses and acts like a man. Her fiancé fights with her and eventually chooses a more submissive woman to marry.

WOODCUTTER   See BAMBOO CUTTER.

Y

YAKAMI (YA-GAMI-HIME)   A beautiful princess who lived in Inaba near IZUMO. See OKUNINUSHI.

YAKUSHI (YAKUSHI-NYORAI)   The BUDDHA of healing, or "master of remedies," Yakushi brings cures for diseases to mankind. As a *bosatsu* or "future Buddha," he dedicated himself to helping humankind and made 12 vows as he worked toward ENLIGHTEN-MENT. One promised to find cures for sickness and disease; another was to light the east.

Yakushi was one of the first Buddhas worshiped in Japan. Art works often show him with a bowl symbolizing his medicine. The bowl is similar to the mortar and pestle once used by European healers to make their medicines.

Yakushi is one of the six Buddhas of meditation. Those devoted to him say he stands in the east, opposite AMIDA, lighting the world.

Yakushi's Sanskrit name is Bhaishajya.

YAMABUSHI   A holy person or hermit who dwells in the mountains and has special powers. In some Japanese legends they associate with TENGU, spirits that live in the mountains and forests. Their magic can be used to heal or to prevent calamities.

YAMATO   The name of the clan that unified Japan in the fourth century and ruled during ancient times. Today's imperial family are direct descendants of these early emperors.

As the Yamato clan grew more powerful, it began to use stories about itself to show others that it had the right to rule. The Shinto CREATION MYTH showed the emperor's direct connection to the most powerful gods that existed. At first, these stories were passed down orally. (See ORAL TRADITION.) Then in the early eighth century, they were written down. *The*

Book of Ancient Things, or the KOJIKI, was recorded around 712. The NIHONGI, which contains much similar material, was written in 720.

The word *Yamato* can be used to mean more than just one family of heroes and kings or the area they came from. It can be seen as the soul or spirit of the country. *Yamato* is used to express the true, core essence of Japan, and as such it existed before the nation itself.

YAMATO-TAKERU (YAMATO TAKE, YAM-ATO DAKE)   In Japanese myth and ancient history, a great warrior and the son of Emperor KEIKO. YAM-ATO is the clan name of the emperors. (It also signifies the area they ruled or, later, Japan, its country and national spirit.)

According to the story laid out in the KOJIKI (*Book of Ancient Things*), Emperor Keiko asked Yamato-Takeru's brother to bring him two beautiful young girls. The young man fell in love with them, married them, and sent other girls in their place.

Angered, the emperor sent Yamato-Takeru to bring his brother back so he could be punished. Instead, Yamato killed his brother, pulling off his arms with his bare hands and crushing him to death.

The emperor was alarmed by his younger son's savage action. However, he also admired his courage and strength. So he sent Yamato to deal with different problems around the kingdom. Yamato went to the palace of two brothers who were rebelling in the south. Yamato dressed as a girl to evade the guards then stabbed the two brothers during the feast.

Until this time, Yamato had been known as O-Usu-No-Ikoto. But one of the dying rebels cried out that his name should be Yamato Takeru—usually translated as "brave Yamato."

Before setting out on a mission to attack rebelling Emishi (natives in the east, probably the people we call ANIU today), Yamato stopped to see an aunt, who gave him a special bag to be used only in an emergency. He also took KUSANAGI, the sword that SUSANO-WO had found in the tail of a DRAGON.

After he had slain many more enemies, Yamato was trapped in a sea of fire. But Yamato used the sword his aunt had given him to cut down the grass. In the bag, he found a flint and set fire to the grass, setting a second fire that put out the first.

Yamato killed many monster SPIDERS, pirates, and the serpent Omi in other adventures. He lost his wife, Oto Tatiban Pime, during a journey when she sacrificed herself to the sea god to calm a storm.

The hero eventually succumbed to a hailstorm that started after he unknowingly threatened a god. His soul changed into a white bird at his death.

YAMA-UBA The goddess of the hunt and forest in SHINTO mythology.

YASAKANI NO MAGATAMA One of the THREE TREASURES given by AMATERASU to her grandson, the first emperor of Japan, in SHINTO myth. Yasakani no Magatama is a necklace made of jewels. The necklace is seen by some scholars as a symbol of fertility. (The other gifts, symbols of the emperor's divinity and power, were a MIRROR and a sword.) The necklace is also known as the *shinshi*.

YASHA A vampire bat. Some believe that the bats are the reincarnated souls of women consumed by anger during their lifetimes.

YATA NO KAGAMI (YATA KAGAMI) According to Japanese myth and tradition, the mirror that made AMATERASU come out of her cave after SUSANO-WO defiled her palace. Yata no Kagami is still possessed by the imperial family and is an important symbol of the emperor. A small mirror is still used as part of the ceremony at a cave commemorating Amaterasu's return.

YAYOI The Yayoi period in Japan dates from roughly 250 B.C. to A.D. 250. It gets its name from the area in TOKYO where anthropologists first discovered a type of pottery different from that made by the earlier people, known to us as the JŌMON culture.

Anthropologists believe that the Yayoi period began after invasions from China to Korea and then Japan. They believe that the newcomers intermingled with the existing people as they brought their art, burial practices, and agriculture to Japan.

Some scholars believe that it was during this time that the imperial family began uniting Japan. Chinese chronicles indicate that toward the end of this period, a "Wo" queen ruled over "Yamatai." *Wo* was the Chinese word for Japan, and Yamatai may be a reference to the YAMATO court. However, there is much debate concerning this interpretation, with many scholars believing that the unification of Japan did not occur until the KOFUN PERIOD, which followed the Yayoi in roughly A.D. 250. (See also HISTORICAL PERIODS.)

YETA A beggar. The god INARI sometimes disguises herself (or himself; the god has both sexes) as a beggar. Because of this, women who seek children are told to give generously to beggars in hopes of pleasing Inari and getting a son.

YIN AND YANG According to ancient Asian philosophy, there are two great opposing forces in the universe. These opposites form the basis for everything. Yin is the female, and yang the male. Yin is cold, yang is FIRE. Known in Japanese as ONMYO, the concept is often symbolized by a circle divided into two opposing swirls, one black, one white.

Scholars say that yin and yang originally referred to the slopes of a mountain that faced away and toward the sun. Some believe that yang was originally a sky god and yin an earth god in China.

The yin-yang idea is an important one in much Chinese mythology and philosophy. The concept is at the heart of the *I Ching (Book of Changes)*, an ancient text that details a system used for fortune-telling.

Besides the philosophical ideas, magic based on the yin-yang principle also traveled from China to early Japan. See CHINESE INFLUENCE.

YO The Japanese equivalent of "yang," or the male half of creation.

YOFUNE-NUSHI According to ancient Japanese myths, a large sea serpent that demanded a maiden to be sacrificed to it every year on June 13. Yofune-Nushi ruled the seas near Oki Island, storming and harassing the fishing fleet. If it did not receive its sacrifice, it would rage, and storms would destroy the fishing fleet.

One year a young girl named TOKOYO volunteered to be sacrificed. She stood on the rocks, waiting for the monster to emerge from its cave below. Yofune-Nushi licked its lips and opened its mouth to eat her. But instead of passively submitting, the girl pulled out a long knife when the sea serpent approached and slashed out its eyes. Stunned, the monster froze, and Tokoyo finished it off with her knife.

YOMI (YOMI-NO-KUNI, YOMI-TSU-KUNI) The netherworld, or land of the dead, in SHINTO myths. The word is translated in different ways in English: "night heart" or "land of darkness" are usual. Yomi is also called Ne no Kuni, or "Land of Roots," and Soko no Kuni, "The Deep Land."

The land of the dead is described in different ways in different myths, and so it is difficult to picture. In the SHINTO CREATION MYTH, Izanagi unsuccessfully travels to Yomi to seek the return of his wife to the land of the living (see IZANAGI AND IZANAMI). Here it is a horrible place, with demons, maggots, and other ghastly sights. But elsewhere it is more like a Christian purgatory. While it is guarded by monsters, souls there are cleansed, not tortured.

YORIGITŌ The act of communicating or channeling spirits in special rituals. These rites usually involve both a SHAMAN, or spirit medium, and a holy person or someone pure in spirit. While their origins are not clear, scholars believe the rites may have come to Japan from China through early BUDDHISM. They were practiced in Japan from ancient times but were officially discouraged by the government at the end of the 19th century.

The best-known ritual, dating from the ninth century and traced to China, was called the Abisha-hō. Four boys or girls around eight years old, all with markless bodies, prepared themselves for a week. The children kept their bodies pure by eating carefully chosen foods. After a special bath, the children put camphor (a kind of wood) in their mouths and then stood on an altar. Attendants prayed a special mantra and burned incense. The boys or girls could then be asked questions about the future or other things and were believed to respond with the truth. This rite was practiced by both the SHINGON and TENDAI sects of BUDDHISM, and there are accounts of emperors using it to answer questions about their reign.

YORIMASA According to Japanese legend, the hero Yorimasa killed a monster that lurked on the top of the emperor's palace. As a reward, he was allowed to marry Lady Ayame and received a sword called Shishi-O, or "Master of Lions."

YORITOMO (MINAMOTO YORITOMO) (1147–1199) The leader of the MINAMOTO clan, which defeated the TAIRA clan in the GEMPEI WAR after an epic struggle during Japan's middle ages. After leading a revolt in 1180, Yoritomo eventually succeeded in becoming SHOGUN, or the military ruler of Japan, at the end of the war in 1185.

As shogun, Yoritomo reestablished order after a period of chaos and war. At times, he ruled with a heavy hand and even fought against his brother YORISUNE. He was succeeded by his widow, Masa-ko, when he died.

YORISUNE (YORIMITSU, YOSHITSUNE, USHIWAKA) (1159–1189) Also known as RAIKO in the legends that followed his death, Yorisune was a real member of the MINAMOTO clan who won fame during the GEMPEI WAR. The younger half-brother of clan leader, YORITOMO, his life became the basis for many stories.

The historical Yorisune's father, Yoshitomo, was killed by a member of the rival TAIRA clan. Still a young man, Yorisune swore revenge. His half-brother Yoritomo let him lead the Minamoto army at Ichinotani. Yorisune won a great victory, charging down a cliff to start a rout of the enemy forces. He then led the army at Dan-no-ura (Dannoura) in 1185, winning a great battle that sealed the fate of the Taira clan.

Yoritomo and Yorisune soon squabbled. Yorisune was eventually apprehended after he tried to escape northward. He and his men killed themselves to preserve their honor.

Yorisune's story is told in several places, including the romance *Gikeiki*. Among his more glorious foes were a giant who continued to fight after his head was chopped off and an enchanted SPIDER.

YOSEI Fairies. Humans see these spirits as birds, cranes, and swans.

YOSHO A Buddhist holy man whose spirit survives and helps people in need.

YUKI-ONNA The Winter Ghost, also known as the Lady of the Snow and the Snow Queen in Japanese myth and folktales. Yuki-Onna can appear in earthly form and can even marry and have children. But she is known to disappear in a white mist at times.

Z

ZAŌ A *BOSATSU* (future BUDDHA) associated with Mount Mitake. According to legend, Zaō helped the holy man E no Uasoku as he subdued demons in the area near Mount Mitake in Saitama Prefecture. Part of the tale is included in the *KONJAKU*.

ZEN BUDDHISM Of the many forms of BUDDHISM practiced around the world, Zen Buddhism is probably the form most often identified with Japan in the West. While certainly popular, it is not numerically the largest sect of the religion followed there. Experts estimate that Zen Buddhism accounts for about 10 percent of Buddhists in Japan.

Zen—or Ch'an (Chan)—was brought first to China by the Indian teacher Bodhidharma (ca. 440–528). Zen first flourished in Japan during the 13th century, despite facing initial opposition from other sects. From its early roots, Zen included martial arts such as archery. As it grew, Zen influenced arts such as painting and poetry.

Zen followers believe that ENLIGHTENMENT can be achieved in a sudden dramatic moment, called *satori*. They place great value in meditation, rather than what we might call book learning. Often, Zen teachers use devices such as koans, paradoxical sayings, to provide a meditation aid for students.

Zen has become so popular in the West that the word *zen* is sometimes used as an adjective on its own, often to mean the "essence" or "spiritual way" of a thing.

ZENKŌ-JI An important Japanese Buddhist TEMPLE in Nagano. According to ancient belief, touching a key in a special passage below the temple will lead to paradise in the afterlife. The temple is extremely popular with Japanese visitors.

ZŌCHŌ-TEN (ZOCHO, ZŌJŌTEN) One of the four HEAVENLY KINGS or SHI TENNŌ. Zōchō-ten guards the south.

MAJOR SHINTO GODS AND GODDESSES

The following Shinto gods and goddesses (not including emperors) have entries in this book:

Aji-Shiki
Aji-Suki-Taka-Hi-Kone
Ama-No-Minaka-Nushi
Amaterasu
Ama-Tsu-Mara
Ame-No-Hohi
Ame-No-Mi-Kumari
Ame-No-Oshido-Mimi
Ame-No-Wakahiko
Am-No-Tanabta-Hime
Atago-Gongen
Chimata-no-kami
Dosojin
Ebisu
Ekibiogami
Fujin
Funadama
Futsu-Nushi-no-Kami
Hachiman
Haniyasu-hiko
Haniyasu-hime
Haya-Ji
Ha-Yama-Tsu-Mi
Hikohohodemi

Hinokagutsuchi
Hiruko
Ho-Masubi
Honosuseri
Hoso-no-Kami
Iha-Naga
Ika-Zuchi-no-Kami
Iki-Ryo
Inari
Izanagi
Izanami
Kagutsuchi
Kamado-no-Kami
Kami-kaze
Kami-Musubi
Kaminari
Kanayama-hiko
Kanayama-hime
Kawa-no-Kami
Kishi-Bojin
Kishijoten
Kojin
Kompira
Koshin

Koya-no-Myoin
Kukunochi-no-Kami
Kura-Okami
Kusa-nada-hime
Masaka-Yama-Tsu-Mi
Mawaya-no-kami
Mizuhame-no-Mikoto
Musubi-no-Kami
Nakatsu-Hime
Naka-Yama-Tsu-Mi
Nakisawame
Ninigi-no-mikoto
Nominosukune
O-Ana-Mochi
Ohonamochi
Oho-Yama
Okuninushi
Omitsuno
Onamuji
O-Yama-Tsu-Mi
Ryujin
Sambo-kojin
Sarutahiko Ohkami
Sengen-Sama

Shigi-Yama-Tsu-Mi
Shina-Tsu-Hiko
Shitatera-Hime
Susano-Wo
Takami-Musubi
Take-Miazuchi
Taki-Tsu-Hiko
Tatsuta-Hiko
Tatsuta-Hime
Tenjin
Toyotama
Toyo-Uke-Bime
Toyouke-Omikami
Tsukiyomi
Tsukiyomo
Uga-no-Mitama
Ukemochi
Uzume
Wakahiru-me
Wata-tsu-mi
Yama-Uba
Yofune-Nushi

MAJOR BUDDHIST DEITIES

The following Buddhist deities have entries in this book:

Aizen-Myō-ō	Fukaotsu	Kannon	Senju Kannon
Amida	Fuku-kensaku Kannon	Kichijōten	Shitennō
Ashuku-Nyorai	Gakkō	Kishimo-jin	Sho Kannon
Bato Kannon	Gozanze-Myō-ō	Kōmoku-ten	Shoki
Benten	Gundari-Myō-ō	Kongo-yasha-Myō-ō	Shoten
Bishamon	Hosho Nyori	Kozuko Bosatsu	Soko
Buddha	Ida-Ten	Kujaku-Myō-ō	Taishaku
Dai-itoku Myō-ō	Jikoku-ten	Mara	Tamon-ten
Dainichi	Jizō	Marishi-Ten	Yakushi
Emma-O	Juichimen	Miro	Zaō
Fudō	Juntei	Monju-Bosatsu	Zōchō-ten
Fugen	Jurojin	Sannō	

SELECTED BIBLIOGRAPHY

Beasley, W. G. *The Japanese Experience*. Berkeley: University of California Press, 1999.

Blacker, Carmen. *Japan Library: The Catalpa Bow*. Surrey, United Kingdom: Curzon Press Ltd., 1999.

Dresser, Christopher. *Traditional Arts and Crafts of Japan*. New York: Dover Publications, 1994.

Graves, Robert, et al. *New Larousse Encyclopedia of Mythology*. New York: Prometheus Press, 1974.

Leach, Maria, and Jerome Fried, eds. *Funk & Wagnalls Standard Dictionary of Folklore, Mythology and Legend*. New York: Harper Collins, 1984.

Leeming, David. *A Dictionary of Asian Mythology*. New York: Oxford University Press, 2001.

Littleton, C. Scott, ed. *Eastern Wisdom*. New York: Henry Holt, 1996.

Mackenzie, Donald A. *Myths of China and Japan*. New York: Gramercy Books, 1994.

McAlpine, Helen, and William McAlpine. *Tales from Japan*. New York: Oxford University Press, 2002.

McCullough, Helen Craig, trans. *Genji & Heike*. Stanford, Calif.: Stanford University Press, 1994.

Milidge, Judith, ed. *Japanese Gods and Myths*. Edison, N.J.: Chartwell Books, 1998.

Mizuno, Kōgen. *Essentials of Buddhism*. Tokyo: Kōsei Publishing, 1996.

Okudaira, Hideo. *Emaki: Japanese Picture Scrolls*. Rutland, Vt.: Charles E. Tuttle Company, 1962.

Simpkins, Annellen M., and C. Alexander Simpkins. *Zen Around the World*. Rutland, Vt.: Charles E. Tuttle Co., 1997.

Storm, Rachel. *Asian Mythology*. New York: Lorenz Books, 2000.

INDEX

Page numbers in **boldface** indicate main entries; page numbers followed by *f* indicate illustrations.